Physical Handicap

A guide for the staff of social services
departments and voluntary agencies

Lesley Bell
Specialist Officer, Services for the Disabled,
London Borough of Waltham Forest

and

Astrid Klemz
Specialist Officer for the Visually Handicapped,
London Borough of Waltham Forest

WOODHEAD-FAULKNER · CAMBRIDGE

First published in 1981,
International Year of Disabled People,
by Woodhead-Faulkner Ltd,
8 Market Passage, Cambridge CB2 3PF

ISBN 0 85941 134 6 (Cased)
ISBN 0 85941 171 0 (Paper)

Phototypeset by Input Typesetting Ltd

Printed in Great Britain by Biddles of Guildford

Preface

This book has been written in response to the many requests for information the authors have received from newly qualified social workers, social work assistants, day care and residential staff, home helps and others who have wanted to know more about ways of helping their handicapped clients. People in health, education and voluntary agencies will find the book a useful guide to the work done by social services departments with handicapped people.

It is a book primarily about rehabilitation, about helping physically handicapped people to realise their full potential, however severe their disability. Self-help, choice and realism are the main subjects emphasised in a wide range of practical information provided for staff as they work with their clients.

Part One of the book describes, in plain terms, the diseases and disabilities commonly met with by social services staff. Part Two gives information on social security benefits, welfare legislation, the duties of social services and central government departments and an outline of the help offered by the major voluntary bodies. Part Three describes the needs of disabled people and aids, adaptations and other possible solutions to the problems involved. Part Four is concerned with rehabilitation centres, employment services, housing needs and recreational facilities. Attention is paid to the difficulties disabled people find when other people do not accept them, and to the problems faced by parents bringing up a handicapped child.

Throughout the book the disabled person, for convenience, is presumed to be male, and the helper to be female, except in Chapter 18 on sexual problems where this is inappropriate.

The authors, both of whom are currently working in a

London Borough social services department and specialise in the field of handicap, hope that this will prove to be a useful handbook for all those working with physically handicapped people.

January 1981   Lesley Bell
                                                Astrid Klemz

Acknowledgements

We are indebted to the following people for their help: Dr J. R. Hayter of Langthorne Hospital, for advice on the medical chapters; Maggie Convery, Specialist Paediatric Occupational Therapist, for her advice on physical handicap in children; Mary Edwards, for reading and commenting on the text; and Mrs G. E. Day, who typed the manuscript. Thanks are also due to the many social services staff who contributed unknowingly by asking questions and demanding answers.

The extract from Stephen Mattingly's *Rehabilitation Today* which appears on p. 202 is reproduced by kind permission of the author and the publishers, Update Books Ltd. We are grateful to the following organisations for their assistance with the preparation of the text illustrations: the Disabled Living Foundation; Carters Ltd; Dantoll Ltd; Homecraft Supplies Ltd; Mecanaids; Nottingham Medical Equipment Company; Possum Controls Ltd; Surgical Medical Laboratory Manufacturing Ltd; and Wessex Medical Equipment Company Ltd.

Finally, we wish to thank our husbands for putting up with the inevitable upheaval while the book was being written.

L. B.
A. K.

Contents

Contents

Part Three: The personal needs of physically handicapped people

Part Four: Provision for physically handicapped people

PART ONE

Common causes of physical handicap

1 Diseases of the joints

It is true to say that all disease by its very nature disables in some way, either temporarily or permanently. However, the diseases which are most commonly encountered by social services staff in their clients are usually those which are of a more permanent nature and have their effect upon the loco-motor system, nervous system and chest and heart. These are the diseases which most often interfere with a normal way of life and the most common of them are described in this and the following chapters, together with their most handicapping effects upon the sufferer. They cause pain, stiffness, weakness or immobility in varying degrees and with these symptoms a sense of helplessness and disability which has an effect upon the person himself, his family and all those with whom he comes into contact (including his social worker!).

Diseases of the connective tissue – that is, the soft tissue sheathing the joints – are responsible for much temporary and permanent disablement. Rheumatic complaints are second only to accidents as regards the number of people affected and second only to bronchitis in the number of working days lost. Added to this, there is a very high proportion of people over working age who suffer from arthritis in varying degrees and therefore it is easy to understand that nearly ten per cent of the work of family doctors is devoted to the diagnosis and treatment of musculo-skeletal disorders grouped under the term "rheumatism".

Rheumatoid arthritis and osteoarthrosis are by far the most common disorders in this category, causing pain, stiffness, weakness and immobility.

Rheumatoid arthritis

Rheumatoid arthritis is a chronic disease affecting all joints, mainly the most peripheral: that is, the fingers and toes, wrists and ankles. It is an incurable disease characterised by periods of acute disability and pain followed by periods of remission, the acute phases being accompanied by general bodily disturbances. The disease is characterised by swelling of the synovial membrane, which sheathes and lubricates the joint, and there is wearing away of cartilage and bone and wasting of the muscles surrounding the joint.

The cause is not known but it is suspected that it may well arise as a result of a number of factors. It used to be believed that the disease was more common in temperate climates associated with cold and damp, though surveys of the populations of sub-tropical regions have shown that rheumatoid arthritis is as common there, although it tends to be less severe. The influence of heredity is not known but a family history of the disease is not infrequently discovered. Women are affected two or three times more often than men, even in the younger age groups, and there is evidence that the disease is very often precipitated or aggravated by emotional disturbances or excessive and long-continued overwork and worry.

In typical cases the small joints of the fingers and toes are the first to become affected. As the disease progresses it spreads to involve the wrists, elbows, shoulders, ankles and knees, but only in the most severe cases are the hips affected. The neck also is commonly involved. Pain and muscular stiffness are characteristic symptoms particularly in the morning and after periods of inactivity.

During the active phase of the disease there is inflammation, pain, swelling and a hotness round the joint and it is at this time that rest is essential, especially in the weight-bearing joints (hips, knees and ankles), to allow the symptoms of inflammation to subside more quickly. The joints are often splinted in the "resting" position to prevent deformity.

When pain and swelling have subsided, splints are removed and active exercises which do not overstrain the limbs are prescribed. The person is instructed to perform these exercises frequently throughout the day whilst not bearing weight on the legs.

Many people who suffer from rheumatoid arthritis never

become severely disabled, as the disease often runs a mild course and can be kept under control by drugs which reduce inflammation and pain. Physiotherapy and remedial exercise may do a great deal towards maintaining a good functional level. For those people, however, who suffer the full, progressive effects of rheumatoid arthritis, when every joint can be affected, the future holds a lifetime of disability.

Modern methods of joint surgery, including replacement of joints with artificial ones, have helped a great deal to prevent people from becoming totally immobile and wheelchair bound. However, if all else fails, life in a wheelchair should be made as purposeful as possible by maintaining whatever useful function the person may have.

Approach to people with rheumatoid arthritis

It is helpful for the person to know that you understand the symptoms which he is experiencing, especially the extent of his pain and the difficulties experienced through muscular spasms, stiffness and weakness. Emotional crisis and depression often occur through prolonged periods of pain and immobility and it is essential for the person to find some positive ways, however small, whereby he can continue in daily living activities and not feel totally helpless. These activities might be preparing vegetables, dressing, dusting, personal grooming, sometimes using aids if need be, or any activity which encourages personal independence and can be achieved.

The family is invariably affected by the depression experienced by the sufferer and his gradually changing role within his family. For example, a housewife may have to relinquish household tasks which are taken over by other members of the family either willingly or reluctantly, sometimes with resulting conflict. The person may be unable to continue working either temporarily or permanently, leading to considerable changes in the family's lifestyle and financial status.

Because there is no complete cure for the disease the person is often told that nothing more can be done for him after drug treatments are given and exercises and general management are explained. This means that life must go on in the knowledge that no great improvement can be expected and a state of "disability" has arrived.

Adjustment to an altered way of living is necessarily a gradual and often a difficult task, and support, encouragement and understanding are required from the social worker, together with the ability to offer advice aimed at extending independence both in practical terms and in social and recreational ways. This is never more appropriate than at the time when a wheelchair is introduced as the only way to achieve mobility in and around the home. The psychological effect of becoming wheelchair bound is profound and will be explored more fully in Chapter 16.

The management of those most severely affected by rheumatoid arthritis is described in Chapter 13.

Osteoarthrosis

Osteoarthrosis is characterised by degeneration of the cartilage covering the movable parts of joints, known as the articular cartilage, and the formation of bony outgrowths at the edges of the affected joints. Usually only one or two of the larger weight-bearing joints, the hips and knees, are involved. Osteoarthrosis affects mainly elderly people of both sexes, although it may appear at any age in a joint which has been damaged by disease or injury. It arises as a result of an exaggeration of the normal ageing process in the joints. Symptoms are prone to develop in weight-bearing joints and in those joints subjected to excessive strain, in particular those of obese people. Symptoms do not often appear before the age of 50.

The articular cartilage splits at the points of maximum weight-bearing and the underlying bone is exposed and becomes denser and harder. New bone is laid down at the edges of the joint. Bony ankylosis, that is, fusion of the joint, never occurs as it can in rheumatoid arthritis, but limitation of movement, "creaking" and the sensation of bone grinding upon bone is experienced. The symptoms are usually very gradual in onset and the pain is of an aching nature and is often intermittent. Movement becomes gradually more limited and there is wasting of muscles surrounding the joint because they are not being used effectively. It is therefore important to move about a little and often.

In the majority of people the disease is confined to one or two joints, especially the hips and knees. Osteoarthrosis differs from rheumatoid arthritis in that it is not inflammatory and therefore not prone to such acute episodes, but osteoarthrotic changes can occur in long-standing cases of rheumatoid arthritis, particularly in the hips and knees.

Treatment of the disease will depend upon the social circumstances of the person and whether undue stress and strain can be removed from the affected joints. The most important single form of treatment in obese people is the reduction of weight so that the legs have less weight to carry. Strenuous work and hobbies may need to be avoided if possible and where pain is severe rest in bed is required temporarily, combined with the local application of heat by such means as hot baths, hot water bottles and woollen knee supports. Gentle active exercises are recommended. Gentle movement of the joints under water relaxes spasm of muscles, diminishes pain and increases the range of movement. Many people do feel better after swimming providing that it is not too strenuous and the water is warm.

Joint replacement is increasingly successful in osteoarthrosis of hips and knees, even in people over 70 years of age. In some cases where only one hip or knee is affected, the joint may be surgically fixed to render it stable and pain-free. However, understandably, this can only be performed in one leg, since the resulting stiff joint can be difficult to manage in sitting down on toilet, armchair or bed or in climbing steps.

Approach to people with osteoarthrosis

Although the pain of osteoarthrosis in joints is not usually experienced with quite the same severity as in rheumatoid arthritis, the resulting stiffening of joints, weakening of muscles and gradual slowing down of walking can cause an equal severity of frustration. If you have once seen an elderly person getting up from a chair so very slowly and with such stiffness that it conjures up the picture of a slow motion film, then you can imagine the difficulties of all activities conducted at so slow and arduous a pace. Walking, leaning on a frame, each foot moving inches at a time, emphasises the difficulty of getting to the toilet before it is too late, or getting to the front door before the caller has gone away.

These are the problems of the person with severe osteoarthrosis, and ones to be helped by practical measures wherever possible. There is often a danger of the affected leg giving way due to weakness of muscles, with the result that falls can be frequent and likely to have serious consequences in fractured bones. Following fractures treated in hospital by surgery, for example, pinning the femur, the person may experience an even greater degree of stiffness and weakness. Walking needs to be encouraged frequently to prevent this, but it must be walking with safety. The removal of worn carpets is often essential to remove hazards. One lady had fallen once on each rug in each room of her house, the offending rug being very reluctantly removed each time!

2 Diseases of the nervous system

Diseases affecting the nervous system are often difficult to diagnose. Often several consultations are necessary before the doctor can say exactly what is wrong with the patient. Both symptoms and the history of the disease have to be taken into account before the doctor can put a name to the condition.

Disorders which arise suddenly, causing maximum disability within a few hours, stay the same for days or weeks and then slowly improve are usually due to strokes (cerebro-vascular accidents), which are dealt with separately in the next chapter. Head injuries can give rise to very similar symptoms, though there is usually a history of accident and signs of injury to the patient.

Disabilities of slow onset which become more severe as time goes on are usually due to some degenerative disease such as cerebral arteriosclerosis (hardening of the arteries) or to tumours within the brain or spinal cord. A remittent history when episodes of disability are followed by improvement with later recurrence of symptoms elsewhere in the nervous systems is characteristic of disseminated (multiple) sclerosis.

Infections, such as poliomyelitis or meningitis, develop their symptoms rapidly. Patients show signs of acute illness and the recovery phase is also more rapid than in vascular accidents or head injuries (although there may, of course, be some remaining disability).

Some conditions are characterised by sudden short-lived disorders of function followed by rapid and complete recovery. A history of this type may be due to epilepsy or migraine or to passing ischaemic attacks (blackouts).

These general principles are a useful guide to the doctor's diagnosis of neurological disorders. It should be borne in

9

mind, however, that there are degrees of severity of symptoms and also individual differences between people with the same condition. The most commonly encountered diseases are described briefly here together with their effect upon the sufferer.

Head injuries

Head injuries can be caused by a blow to the head, either with or without a fracture of the skull, and should in all cases be treated seriously even if the person admits to "feeling fine" immediately afterwards. Head injuries can also be caused by a very sudden jolt such as is commonly experienced nowadays by a passenger in a stationary car when the car is suddenly hit by the car behind. This is called a "whiplash" injury. In both cases the damage is caused by the brain hitting the bony skull with force.

Symptoms may come on immediately, when the person is knocked unconscious, or gradually, when after several hours or even days he begins to experience what are called post-concussional symptoms. There may be headache, dizziness associated with bending down or turning the head, vomiting, difficulty in concentration, mental fatigue and increased anxiety and sometimes depression. In cases where the brain has been badly damaged there may be similar symptoms to stroke illness – that is, dysphasia, dysarthria, hemianopia and other difficulties of vision, hemiplegia and epileptic-type fits. The patient often recovers gradually from these symptoms as swelling and pressure within the brain reduces but in some cases permanent damage to the brain gives rise to some residual disability.

Approach to people after head injuries

The social worker will usually be concerned with two types of people after they have sustained a severe head injury.

One type is the person who appears physically fit and well but displays disturbances of memory, lack of concentration, personality changes, including moodiness or emotional lability, depression and anxiety neurosis. Often this person is unable to return to his former employment or has to be re-employed in the same firm in a different capacity, owing to his impaired memory and concentration. Such a person usually experiences difficulties with previously harmonious family relationships and the strains upon the family can be very great, both emotionally and economically. These stresses are particularly severe when there are aggressive outbursts in a previously calm person, overt sexual expression or sudden changes in moods.

Treatment will involve training the person to deal with lapses in memory and to improve concentration, and the possible retraining for an alternative type of employment. Such treatment will usually take place within a hospital occupational therapy department, a medical rehabilitation centre or in the various kinds of government work assessment and training centres. The local Disablement Resettlement Officer (DRO) will be able to advise on a suitable programme of work retraining. More importantly, support for the person and his family is needed in order that they may be able to adjust their lives. In cases where severe personality changes are present, psychiatric help may be needed, as well as periods of relief for the family in whatever ways are locally possible.

The other type of disability which may remain after a head injury is when the person has sustained permanent severe damage to the brain and spinal cord and is consequently permanently paralysed in all limbs. This person may be nursed at home by a caring family, when practical help is needed in terms of personal management. The district nurse will usually be attending the person and helping in washing, bowel and bladder control and dealing with problems of pressure sores and the like. The family may need help to lift the person out of bed and generally minister to his daily needs. Some independence may be achievable in feeding and personal activities and in developing interests and leisure activities. More advice is given later in this book.

It must be remembered in all cases that damage to the head has a special effect upon a person, for it is in the head that we feel we reside. It is the centre of the conscious being. If we inhabit our bodies it is in the head that this feeling is situated, the ego, the mind, the personality. We can often divorce ourselves from the rest of our body but not from our head (unless one goes in for "astral projection"!). Feelings of losing the mind are associated with failing memory, concentration and other previously intact mental functions, and so it is an important task to understand what has happened and to help the person to adjust to these changes.

Disseminated (multiple) sclerosis

In order to understand the variety of possible symptoms in multiple sclerosis it is necessary to describe briefly the structure of the central nervous system (Fig. 1).

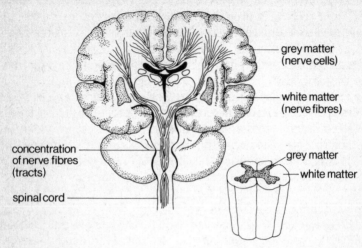

Fig. 1 The brain and central nervous system, with a cross-section of the spinal cord

The central nervous system is made up of grey matter (nerve cells) and white matter (nerve fibres). In the brain the grey matter is on the outside and the white matter on the inside. In the cerebellum, which controls co-ordination of movement, among other things, it is the same. In the spinal cord the reverse structure exists: in a cross section of the spinal cord, the nerve cells are on the inside and the fibres are on the outside.

It is the white matter, the fibres, which is affected in multiple sclerosis – the nerves in the brain, the spinal cord and the optic nerves. Nerves are of two types: sensory, bringing messages to the brain about the condition of the body and world around it, and motor, carrying messages from the brain to effect movement in response to sensory experience.

Multiple sclerosis is called a demyelinating disease. This means loss of the myelin sheaths which encase nerve fibres in the brain and spinal cord. The function of the myelin sheath is to nourish and preserve the nerve fibres and therefore facilitate the smooth conduction of nervous impulses up and down between the body and the brain. When the myelin sheath is destroyed in patches, as in this disease, parts of the nerves gradually die and, because they cannot regenerate themselves, the damage is permanent and the disease is termed progressive. Impulses are conducted less smoothly at first and then with progressive difficulty, so that the resulting loss of movement comes on slowly.

The deterioration of the myelin sheaths is patchy throughout the brain and spinal cord. The peripheral nerves have been found not to be susceptible to the disease and so consequently muscles do not actually waste because there is still muscle tone present. In fact, jerky, spastic contractions may occur in the muscles of the limbs which are thought to be due to interruption of the pathways from the brain itself.

The most characteristic features of multiple sclerosis are the spasmodic, intermittent course of the disease and the widespread locations of damage, causing a corresponding variety of disabilities for the patient, depending on where the damage has occurred.

The initial attack may only cause temporary functional interruption of the nerve fibres which are not permanently damaged and so the early symptoms may often disappear.

The first attack and later relapses can be started by unusual fatigue, trauma, infection, severe cold and allergic reactions. Such events as childbirth or a severe emotional shock may also appear to have been the starting point. It affects people usually between the ages of 20 and 50. It is rarely seen before puberty and seldom appears for the first time after 50. The first symptoms will depend on which parts of the brain or spinal cord are affected but are usually twofold.

1. Blurring of vision or even loss of vision in one eye, with pain on moving the eyeball – most common in younger people.
2. Weakness in both legs. This often presents as a slight clumsiness at first – most common in older adults.

These initial symptoms may disappear within a few days or weeks or they may continue with added problems developing.

After the initial phase has subsided the person may continue to be well for a variable length of time – months or maybe years – until the next relapse. Other symptoms, which may be the intitial ones or others occuring during the relapses, are:

lesions in the brain: transient double vision, acute vertigo and vomiting;

lesions in the cerebellum: inco-ordination of arms; intention tremor of the hands (the hands begin to shake when about to grip or pick up something), unsteadiness in walking, staggering (rather like a drunken walk), dysarthria (difficulty in articulating words);

lesions in the spinal cord: numbness or loss of sensation in the face, body or limbs, disturbance of bladder function (i.e. urgency, precipitancy or hesitancy), impotence, muscle weakness;

mental symptoms: reactive depression is understandably common; occasionally there is a mood of almost excessive cheerfulness, which is called euphoria.

Slight intellectual deterioration is not uncommon in the very latest stages of the disease but dementia is rarely seen.

After each attack the symptoms may subside a little but with each relapse they may recur or there may be fresh symptoms not experienced before. The shorter the time between attacks the more likely, it is thought, that the disease will become progressive.

The course of multiple sclerosis is so variable that in the early stages it is impossible to predict what is going to happen to the patient. Although in some people the disease progresses rapidly, approximately sixty per cent of people are without disability five years after the onset and forty per cent after ten years. The average duration of life is at least twenty years after the onset. Death is usually caused by urinary infection, pneumonia or pressure sores.

Treatment

The cause of multiple sclerosis has not yet been found and therefore there is no real cure as yet. However, an acute attack is sometimes treated with a hormone called ACTH, and some response has been noticed. When an attack has been brought on by a urinary infection then the speedy treatment of this can alleviate the nervous symptoms.

During a bad attack the person is best confined to rest in bed, but not for too long, as muscular co-ordination can be rapidly lost by too much inactivity. Regular activity is essential, avoiding overtiredness on the one hand and too much rest on the other. Physiotherapy and occupational therapy are valuable, providing exercises which improve co-ordination of the use of arms and legs and maintain the performance of activities of daily living. Drugs are used to treat retention or frequency of passing urine.

The psychological effect of the disease is of the utmost importance.

Approach to people with multiple sclerosis

Because multiple sclerosis is popularly known as an incurable disease which is progressive and *can* result eventually in a total loss of normal movement, the name is feared almost as much as "cancer". Therefore, having the diagnosis confirmed can begin an extremely traumatic time for the sufferer, particularly in the event of the diagnosis being made during a bad attack. On the other hand, because there may be improvement after the first attack the person may cling to the hope that there will not be further attacks and that the disease will pass away and he will get better. With this disease, more than most, there is the hope that a cure may be found soon and he will recover completely. A great deal of research is happening at present and any advances hit the headlines almost too quickly, successes often becoming exaggerated in people's minds.

Helping people to continue their normal life as far as possible is of vital importance and when activities become more difficult support in adjusting to alternative ways of functioning is required. The Multiple Sclerosis Society of Great Britain (address given in Chapter 11), with its many active local groups, offers considerable support to its members even when people who are fairly mobile mix with those who are more severely handicapped. However, many people do not turn to the MS Society because they do not wish to accept the self-image of the "disabled person" which can prevail amongst groups of sufferers. It is these people who may require considerable support from social services staff to adjust to new roles amongst family, friends and work colleagues, who are also affected by the label of the disease.

Symptoms which cause the greatest social difficulties and embarrassments are urinary problems, particularly incontinence, and impotence. Sexual problems as well as anxiety, depression and frustration can put extreme strains upon marital relationships and there is a great need for expert marriage counselling for couples who have to live with multiple sclerosis.

Although the euphoria sometimes present can be a godsend to the person himself, it can put a great burden upon the partner who has then to carry the worries of daily life alone.

Families need practical help in the form of adaptations to their home and aids to management such as special beds or hoists, which will take the hard work out of ordinary daily tasks such as getting out of bed and bathing. The marriage partner may need more support than the disabled person himself to cope with the disease. An independent approach to living needs fostering, wherein the person does as much as he can for himself within his capabilities and without tiring himself out. He needs to find a valid role which he can fulfil within his family. Attendance at a day centre for the person can provide vital relief for his partner and holidays in the summer, either together or apart, can help to maintain relationships and recharge emotional batteries.

Time spent in supporting families may need to be continuous over many years and is often essential in maintaining family life. It is regrettable that often there are insufficient staff to undertake long-term social work with families who need it.

Epilepsy

About one in every 200 people suffers some form of epilepsy at sometime in his life. It is by no means an unusual or uncommon disease, and it has been suggested that most people have the potential for epileptic attacks. It is the "sacred disease" of ancient times and was suffered by Julius Caesar (whose fits were possibly brought on by overwork and worry!). It is characterised by seizures or fits, which may occur in different forms. All fits are described as a brief disorder of brain function, usually associated with a disturbance of consciousness and accompanied by a sudden excessive electrical discharge in the nerve cells of the brain. The most frequently seen type of epilepsy is called "idiopathic" epilepsy, because there is no recognisable source of the fits. It presents itself in fits known as "*grand mal*" and "*petit mal*".

Grand mal fit

The most common picture of an epileptic fit is that known as a *grand mal* attack. There are several stages, which are practically without variation in all cases.

1. There is what is called a prodromal phase which may last hours or days. This usually takes the form of a change of mood and warns the person that an attack is pending.
2. There is sometimes an aura immediately before a fit which most commonly takes the form of a peculiar sensation starting in the stomach and spreading up into the throat and head. It can also be a sudden rushing in the head.
3. Next follows the tonic stage when the person loses consciousness. There is a prolonged tensing of all muscles, when the person becomes rigid and falls, often emitting a cry which is caused by the muscles of respiration also contracting and pushing air from the lungs through the tense throat. Breathing stops and the face becomes bluish (cyanosed). This phase lasts about 20–30 seconds.
4. The clonic phase follows, when the rigidity gives way to interrupted, powerful jerking movements of the face, body and limbs. The person can bite his tongue during this phase unless a resilient object is placed between the teeth. He may also be incontinent of urine and, less often, of faeces. These movements are often described as convulsions.
5. After about half a minute the movements stop and the person relaxes in a comatose state which evolves into normal sleep. This may last for a few minutes, or for half an hour or more. After regaining consciousness there may be a variable period of confusion and the person may have a headache.

Petit mal fit

The most common form of *petit mal* attack takes the form of a transient loss of consciousness. The person interrupts what he is doing and stares blankly into space. Such absences may occur in children: this is a period of life when *petit mal* often starts, but it may stop completely during adolescence or change to adult *grand mal* attacks. Sometimes the brief loss of consciousness is accompanied by a jerking of the arms.

Epileptic fits can be brought on by different recognisable stimuli such as flickering lights or emotional disturbances. Other fits, caused by tumours or head injuries, or occurring after strokes, can appear in a variety of ways, according to the site of the damage in the brain. However, they are usually characterised by movements of the body and limbs and some loss of consciousness to a greater or lesser extent. The term *status epilepticus* refers to continuous fits, *grand mal* or *petit mal*, which occur one after the other without pause; this can be very serious and must be treated as soon as possible.

Treatment

Epileptic fits can be controlled by a variety of drugs, although some of them make the person drowsy to a certain extent. It is important that medicines are taken regularly as prescribed. The physician's diagnosis of the cause of the fits is important, because if there is an organic cause such as a tumour, an operation may be indicated. Electroencephalograms (EEG) are used in the diagnosis to record the unusual brain wave patterns present in epilepsy.

If fits are brought on by known stimuli then these must be avoided by the person if possible.

Approach to people with epilepsy

Because of the bizarre and dramatic nature of the epileptic fit, it has been a source of fear through the ages of mankind, and thought to be related to possession by demons and madness. People with the disease thus have been shunned and it is only in recent years that the nature of the fits has been explained. The ordinary population is still afraid of seeing a person having a fit in public and so there has grown up a stigma attached to epilepsy which is second to none except that of mental illness. Employers are loath to take on the epileptic and many normal pursuits are denied once it is known that a person has *grand mal* fits. The British Epilepsy Association has been instrumental in trying to explain the disease to the public and to dispel the fear that epilepsy evokes. Nevertheless we must remember that even if fits are infrequent and controlled a person is still likely to have some difficulty in leading a normal life because of the attitude of others.

The most important approach is to help the epileptic person to recognise the symptoms of an approaching fit so that he may prepare himself for it. If he feels himself to be leading up to a fit, he can take precautions to avoid injuring himself. He may sit or lie down to avoid abruptly falling to the ground and he may take his glasses off or his dentures out of his mouth. Fits often happen during the night and may be so energetic that the person falls out of bed. In this case, cotsides or sturdy furniture placed against the bed may stop this happening and avoid sleepless nights for the rest of the family who have to pick him up off the floor and put him back to bed.

Many people learn to control their fits by careful medication and by avoiding undue stress or the sensory stimuli known to cause them. This is sometimes difficult to do and still lead a normal active life. Regular fits are very disabling and can cause the person to lose confidence in himself and to retreat from contact with others.

If the social worker is confronted by someone having a fit, she should act calmly, remembering the pattern of fits. All she can do is to remove furniture and other objects from around the person so that he will not hurt himself on anything sharp or hard. She should wait for the convulsions to subside and then make the person comfortable on the floor by putting a pillow under the head, covering him if it is cold, and allow him to sleep it off.

The person with epilepsy needs sympathetic and understanding encouragement to seek help, whether from his own doctor or from local voluntary groups which help epileptics. From such groups he will gain support from fellow sufferers when it is needed. The Disablement Resettlement Officer should be approached to help find suitable employment for the epileptic person. He will know of retraining and employment prospects and will be aware of the type of work which is unsuitable.

All in all, a positive attitude is needed which will encourage the person to lead a normal life within his capabilities and encourage other people to accept him without fear of his fits. As with many disabilities, it is the disabled person himself who can make the most impression upon the attitudes of the people that he meets.

The social worker is advised to seek further advice from

the British Epilepsy Association, who will be very willing to give it.

Parkinson's disease (paralysis agitans)

This disease occurs between the ages of 50 and 60 years and is characterised by three main signs:

(a) impaired voluntary movement;
(b) bodily rigidity;
(c) the appearance of involuntary movements (tremor).

The first sign is usually a tremor in one hand called a "pill rolling" movement, because it looks as if the person is rolling a small pill between his thumb and first finger. This tremor may spread to the other hand after months or years. Sometimes the tongue moves and the eyelids close and flicker. The tremor of Parkinson's disease is present when the person is relaxed and resting, usually disappears when he makes a voluntary movement such as picking up something, but starts again when a new position of the hand is adopted. It also disappears during sleep.

As this disease progresses, poverty of movement and rigidity begin to occur. The expressive movements of the face are slowly lost and the expression becomes mask-like giving a false impression of dim-wittedness. Gradually automatic movements of the body such as swinging the arms when walking and the ability to maintain the balance are reduced or lost. The rigidity of the body makes walking difficult and the gait becomes shuffling, with the steps becoming little running movements which may eventually bring the person to a standstill. Turning round is extremely difficult, because this necessitates an alteration of balance as well as controlled turning steps. It is also difficult for the person to initiate voluntary movements such as getting up out of a chair, as the natural spring of that action is reduced by rigidity. Turning over in bed is impossible and this leads to pain and muscular cramps.

Speech may be affected, becoming rapid and monotonous with slurring of consonants and repetition of syllables. Handwriting may become progressively smaller. With concentrated effort movement, speech and writing can often be performed normally for a few moments but when attention is relaxed they deteriorate again.

Treatment

The cause of Parkinson's disease is not known but it has been found that there are chemical changes in the brain, namely the reduction of the amount of a substance called dopamine, which facilitates the transmission of nervous impulses in those parts of the nervous system which help to maintain the rhythm of voluntary movements. Most recent treatment has been to administer synthetically prepared dopamine (L-dopa) and this has been found to produce a significant improvement in many patients. However, it has not been in use for sufficient time for doctors to judge how long it can continue to be beneficial or how it might influence the natural course of the disease.

Speech therapy is often helpful and physiotherapy and occupational therapy can help to train the person to perform the movements necessary to continue his daily life.

Approach to people with Parkinson's disease

It is necessary to appreciate the degree of frustration which the person feels in relation to his disability. Whilst facial expression and speech may be considerably impaired, the person's mind is unaffected and it is essential to approach him normally and not to talk down to him. He feels the same inside despite his inability to smile, frown and perform the many complex movements of his face which help us all to communicate our feelings to people around us. He will have to say in words, if he can, the things he would normally communicate non-verbally. One is often surprised by the humorous and succinct remarks, carefully phrased, which issue from the mask-like exterior.

The sufferer is also likely to be frustrated by his immobility and will need encouragement to concentrate on performing his normal personal activities by finding alternative ways of doing things.

Motor neurone disease

A description of this disease is included because, although it is less common than the previously described disorders, in our experience it accounts for a significant proportion of people being referred to social services departments. These people are often living at home and are progressively deteriorating physically. They require help and support both for

21

themselves and their families in managing the physical and psychological problems associated with this incurable and often rapidly advancing illness.

The disease affects the motor nerves and the cause is unknown. There appears to be a "dying back" of nerves from the muscles to the spinal cord, which some authorities think is due to a biochemical failure of some kind. Consequently, the first signs of the disease are the wasting of the small muscles in the hands, and gradually the wasting spreads up the arms. The legs become affected – first the feet and then gradual weakness of the legs, especially when the person is tired. There may be speech disturbance (dysarthria) because the muscles of speech become affected and swallowing may become increasingly difficult (dysphagia). The muscles of the face may become affected as well. In the last stages of the disease breathing becomes difficult.

The onset of motor neurone disease is usually between the ages of 50 and 70. There is no specific treatment which will halt its course but much can be done to help both patient and family.

Approach to people with motor neurone disease

Social stimulation in the form of day care or short-term residential care can help to alleviate the difficulty of living with this disease.

For a while the person will be able to continue to walk with aids but inevitably he will eventually need to use a wheelchair. Gradually he will need increasing physical support from the chair itself so that the wheelchair at first prescribed may have to be changed for another model giving back, head and leg support.

The physical and psychological effects of such an incurable and deteriorating disease upon a person and his family provides the basis from which the social worker begins. The person needs constant encouragement to maintain independence when this is possible and to accept dependence when it is not. Long-term social work support for families is usually indicated and increasing advice and assistance with practical management, such as lifting, moving and feeding. Short-term relief may be necessary from the daily chores of management, which can become a great burden for relatives.

Spinal injuries

Road traffic accidents and falls from heights account for most spinal injuries today. When the spinal cord is damaged severely, then paralysis of muscles served by the nerves branching out of the spinal cord below the level of the damage occurs. The higher-up the level of injury, the greater the resulting area of paralysis.

The terms paraplegia and quadriplegia describe the varying degrees of disability which can occur as a result of spinal injuries. Paraplegia means paralysis of the lower part of the body, i.e. both legs. Quadriplegia or tetraplegia means paralysis of both legs and both arms. (Hemiplegia will be described in relation to stroke illness. It means paralysis of one side of the body, one leg and one arm, and is not the result of a spinal injury but of a lesion higher up in the brain.)

The greatest damage is done by a severe injury to the upper part of the neck. If the lower part of the neck or the upper part of the back is damaged then the person may retain the use of his arms.

Treatment

The immediate treatment is directed at saving the person's life but after this is done, and the rhythm of bodily processes is stable, then treatment is directed to the care of the skin, the bladder, the bowels, the paralysed muscles, and to rehabilitation.

Skin Pressure sores can very easily develop, due to loss of sensation and reduced blood supply arising out of the person's immobility. He is unable to move himself off his buttocks and heels and does not feel discomfort in these parts. Therefore he must be nursed on antipressure bedding and turned over every few hours, day and night. If sores do develop then these will require careful nursing and skin grafts may be required in severe cases when the sores do not heal. A good nutritional diet is given, containing adequate amounts of protein, vitamin C and iron, as these promote healing.

Bladder Retention of urine often occurs and is treated by regular catheterisation. After that an in-dwelling catheter is used which is attached to a drainage bottle. This can be clipped and allowed to drain at regular intervals to establish

23

a reflex emptying of the bladder. As the rhythm becomes established the catheter is withdrawn and the person trained to pass water at fixed times. Emptying of the bladder can be assisted by pressure with the hands by the person himself on the lower part of his abdomen (if he cannot do this then a relative may be taught to do it for him).

Bowels   Constipation is prevented as far as possible by a suitable diet and laxatives. Some people with quadriplegia may need regular manual evacuation of their bowels by the nurse (this means that the bowel is emptied by hand).

Paralysed muscles   In this type of injury the affected muscles will be inclined to be more excitable and liable to contract more: this is called spasm. The spasm can lead to the limbs contracting up permanently. The resulting deformity is called a contracture.

To prevent contractures occuring the limbs are regularly put through their normal range of movement by the physiotherapist. The person also is positioned in bed so that flexion contractures will not form – for example, permanent flexion of the hips is avoided by placing a pillow under the lower part of the back.

A bed cradle is used to keep the bedclothes from resting on the legs, as their weight can cause the toes to be pressed down and result in a permanent foot drop. The weight of the bedclothes can also stimulate the muscles on the front of the thighs to contract up, so this has to be prevented.

Rehabilitation   More will be said later about rehabilitation. People with paraplegia can return to a full normal life given the opportunity of early, comprehensive rehabilitation. Much relies upon the generation of motivation and enthusiasm in the person himself and this will depend upon the positive attitude of staff in the spinal injuries unit, and an early start to rehabilitation.

Approach to people with spinal injuries

Although it is felt that a description of paraplegia will be useful to the social services worker, in our experience paraplegic people rarely seek help because of their disability. They have retained the use of and learned to strengthen their arms and can therefore move themselves about and retain independence. They are also younger and have an intact brain. We meet them more as voluntary helpers who are leading normal lives and who are motivated to help others in wheelchairs who are less fortunate than themselves. This is mainly because paraplegia due to spinal injury is rarely deteriorating in nature and therefore, once rehabilitated, the individual can be healthy and active once more. His concern is with access, in all senses of the word, to an integrated life. Paraplegics are often the people who have done most to further the cause of disabled people.

It is those that have suffered more extensive paralysis, quadriplegia, who need help when they are discharged home from hospital. They are often tragically young people who have been involved in accidents and whose lives are completely changed. They and their families need considerable help to build a new life, often in a new environment, because much adaptation of the physical environment at home is required to facilitate the maximum functioning of both patient and family. Alongside the physical help comes the psychological restructuring and such families usually require long-term social work help towards the gradual rebuilding of their lives.

In our experience the early intervention, following the person's discharge from hospital, of both social worker and occupational therapist is vital to help both client and family through the first few months of this most traumatic time. The occupational therapist is able to provide advice on necessary equipment and structural alterations to the home and on management of the total physical situation. The social worker is vital in supporting the person and his family and helping them to come to terms with the reality of the situation and to adapt to the many difficulties, both physical and emotional. This requires of the social worker considerable skills in casework but too often, sadly, this type of case is allocated to the relatively unskilled social work assistant.

3 Strokes

Of every thousand people suffering a stroke, a half will die soon after, and a third will do well, but of this third a large proportion will return home with the residual problem of a useless arm. The remainder will stay in the community but be severely disabled and need care, either from relatives or in residential homes. Some may have to be nursed in long-stay hospital.

Strokes are caused by vascular disturbances which result in an interruption of blood supply, and therefore nourishment, to the brain. There may be haemorrhage into brain tissues causing pressure, thrombosis (blood clot in the blood vessels) or embolism (another type of obstruction). There is often a loss of consciousness, either momentary or continuing, followed by the development of paralysis.

Damage of this kind to one side of the brain produces paralysis on the opposite side of the body (hemiplegia) since the paths of nerves from the brain to the muscles cross in a lower part of the brain. Thus, damage on the left side of the brain produces loss of function on the right side of the body.

The speech area in a right-handed person is situated on the left side of the brain and therefore right-sided paralysis usually goes with a speech disorder. This will be described later.

Early treatment

Severe strokes are best treated in hospital, where a skilled team of doctor, nurse, physiotherapist, speech therapist and occupational therapist are on hand to help the patient achieve as much recovery as is possible. However, many people suffering strokes at home never get to hospital and it is the family doctor and the district nurse who manage the early treatment

26

and rehabilitation. In some areas of the country domiciliary physiotherapists join them to help in the rehabilitation process, as does also the community occupational therapist. Speech therapy at home is still a rare commodity, but no less essential, and so often the person has to attend a speech therapy clinic as an out-patient. At home, and increasingly in hospitals also, the relatives are considered part of the treatment team, as they have to carry on the work of rehabilitation continually throughout the day.

Medical treatment of a stroke will depend upon the cause diagnosed by the doctors but will often involve control of high blood pressure and of diabetes. It may also be thought advisable to reduce the ability of the blood to clot by using anticoagulants or aspirin. The nursing of the unconscious patient is aimed at keeping airways clear, avoiding respiratory infection, making sure that pressure sores do not develop, looking after bowel and bladder and providing fluid and food by tube.

Strokes can be divided into three types:

1. Complete – when the patient is seen for the first time the stroke is complete. It has happened and the body is ready to settle down to a stable condition.
2. Continuing – when the patient is seen for the first time the stroke is continuing: no stable condition has been reached yet.
3. Stuttering – when the patient is first seen the stroke is neither complete or continuing and it is said to be stuttering (this is sometimes described as repeated small strokes).

The outlook for the complete stroke is good, whereas for the continuing and stuttering strokes it is poor.

Rehabilitation

When the person is conscious and his bodily condition reasonably stable, then active rehabilitation can begin. The following areas of disability may be noticed.

Complete loss of balance on the affected (paralysed) side of the body

This happens because the patient has lost his normal postural reflex mechanism, the automatic movements which retain balance against gravity. A baby develops this mechanism as it

27

rolls on the floor and progresses to crawling, sitting and standing. This mechanism has to be re-educated after a stroke to prevent the person flopping over to the affected side and help him to balance when standing and walking. It is sometimes called the "righting" reflex, meaning that it enables the person automatically to keep an upright position when moving.

Disturbance of the sensation of bodily position

The position of the body and the way it moves is in direct response to the body's knowing where it is situated in space. This is done through messages sent to the brain from sensory nerve ends in every muscle and joint describing its position, in relation to other parts of the body and to gravity. If you close your eyes and raise your right arm above your head, you know that that is where your arm is. If you hold it there, you know not only that you put it there, but that that *is* its position. If you now move it straight out to the side of your body, you still know just where it is. This is because sensory messages are being sent to your brain telling you of the position of your arm.

The person with a sensory disturbance would not know the position of his arm and he would "lose" it. This kind of sensory disturbance can be a most crippling disability. However, in some people suffering from stroke it is only slight. It should be acknowledged that it is present, nevertheless, so that we understand why the patient cannot always control the movements and position of his body.

Developing spasm in the muscles

For every movement there is an opposite movement. We bend the arm up to the face, and we straighten the arm away from the face. All movements are achieved by the contraction of muscles. Muscles on the inner side of the elbow make it bend and those on the outside make it straighten. In the normal body usually one group of muscles is stronger than the other. In the legs, those muscles which keep the leg straight (to support the body when standing) are the strongest; in the arm, the strongest muscles are those that bend the arm for carrying and against gravity. Therefore, in stroke, when muscles go into spasm – that is, when they contract automatically without conscious instruction – it is the extensors of the legs and the flexors of the arms which contract. This is called spasm.

This can be useful in that the legs need to be straight to bear the weight of the body for walking, but it can be extremely hampering in both legs and arms when they will not move in the opposite direction in response to conscious commands from the brain. Skilled physiotherapy can help to avoid increasing spasm.

Complete loss of free selection of movements

It is not surprising that in the presence of the preceding three problems the person suffering from stroke cannot perform selected movements when he wants. He may desire to extend his arm to reach something but, no matter how much he wants to do this, he cannot make his arm obey. It is therefore essential that his treatment in hospital be towards re-educating his position sense, balance and sensation.

This rehabilitation is skilled and is performed from the earliest possible moment by rehabilitation team of nurse, physiotherapist and occupational therapist. There are, however, ways in which other workers caring for the person can help in the practice and re-education of movements. If you have in your care such a patient, then it is recommended that you seek the advice of a physiotherapist or occupational therapist who will teach you how to manage him, helping him towards maximum independence rather than doing everything for him.

Hemianopia

Hemianopia is a condition in which the person loses half the field of vision in each eye. For example, the person with hemianopia often only sees one half of his dinner plate. He eats all the food on the left side of the plate unaware that there is more on the right side of the plate. When asked if the plate is empty he replies that it is. This disability can sometimes be minimised by teaching the person to turn his head to the right so that he can see that side of his plate. However, in severe cases of perceptual loss, training is not possible.

Speech disorders in stroke

There are two types of speech disorder:

1. Dysarthria   This is the more simple type and often clears up, at least to a certain extent. It is a disorder in speaking due to the loss of muscular control of the tongue, lips, mouth and throat. There is no reading or language problem. Exercises given by the speech therapist are aimed at re-educating the mechanics of speech and building up words and phrases. Dentures must fit and hearing aids must work. Eyesight may also need to be checked. Writing may be difficult due to weakness of the dominant hand or the person having to learn to write with his other hand.

2. Dysphasia or, when complete, aphasia We have said that the effect of a stroke on the left side of the brain produces a paralysis on the right side of the body and vice versa. In a right-handed person the centre in the brain which controls speech is usually situated on the left side of the brain and therefore in the case of right-sided paralysis there is almost always a speech disorder. In those people who are left-handed, a left-sided paralysis may be accompanied by speech disturbance. Dysphasia is a disorder of language which may include understanding, speaking, reading and writing. There are three types of dysphasia: expressive, receptive and mixed.

In *expressive dysphasia* comprehension of the spoken and written word remains comparatively intact but it is the person's ability to find words to express himself which is hampered. He may speak slowly, searching for words and often getting the wrong ones (which he knows are wrong). When word finding is very difficult perseveration can be present: that is, the constant repetition of one word, getting stuck to the word.

It is important for the person talking to him to know his background and interests so that he can be encouraged to talk about the things he knows. A favourite magazine or newspaper might be produced. Plenty of time is needed for the person to find the words and reassurance should be given that his difficulty is understood. Helping with words is only useful in moderation, for if this is constantly done it does not allow the person to find the word for himself and then only builds up frustration. Putting words into the mouth is even more frustrating, as we have all found from experience at some time!

With *receptive dysphasia* comprehension is missing and the person does not understand the spoken or written word. It is usually associated with a loss of position sense of the right side (or the dominant side) of the body and with hemianopia (both referred to earlier).

The speech may be fluent but incomprehensible. The guidance of the speech therapist is essential in this type of speech disorder and she will be concerned with training auditory discrimination of words.

Mixed dysphasia is when both expression and comprehension are lost. The breakdown in verbal communication has a profound effect upon a person. The person's whole way of life is threatened because of his lack of communication with his family and others. He sees himself as useless and worthless and may withdraw from any participation, becoming depressed, bad-tempered, frustrated and generally labelled as difficult and frequently unpleasant. It is important to realise the severity of this disability.

There is a tendency for us to consider the loss of speech also as a loss of intelligence and the person in the early stages of his illness must be given the benefit of the doubt. He should be considered to be able to understand everything which is said to him and not be insulted by the careless habit of talking across him as if he does not understand.

The patient will be bewildered and frightened and therefore he must be reassured continually, told where he is, what has happened to him and what is to be done to help him. Asking him to continually repeat words and phrases will only build up his anxiety and frustration and make improvement in his speech impossible to achieve.

It is important to check first that false teeth are fitting well and hearing is unimpaired; referral for a hearing aid may be needed. It is also important to make sure that glasses are used if usually worn.

Speech rehabilitation is a skilled job and best left to the speech therapist; however, she will be able to guide you and the family through the methods of communication which will help the rehabilitation process. The golden rules are:

(*a*) reassure constantly (positively not sentimentally);
(*b*) don't aggravate frustration;
(*c*) don't insist on repetition of simple words and phrases;
(*d*) don't isolate the patient but allow him to join others in a group;

(*e*) don't lose contact with him.

It is most important in all language disorders for contact to be maintained with the person by professional workers, family and friends. Plenty of information about the person's background and interests is needed in order to keep up conversation. Alternative means of communication, such as gestures and miming are also useful. Every possible means of communication should be used to maintain contact; this may mean the establishment of a totally non-verbal language. Rapport and mutual understanding are all-important.

Stroke clubs

Stroke clubs have been set up in many areas by speech therapists. They may take place on hospital premises but are most effective when held within the community, in health centres, church halls and the like. The aim of such a club is to bring together families with a member who has had a stroke where a speech disorder has been sustained.

The stroke club provides support for the person and his relatives and a group where communication can be practised and heightened and where relatives can learn from each other of the varied methods of communication which others find successful. Very often social workers and occupational therapists attend the clubs regularly, for they may pick up other problems which people might need help in solving.

The profound effect on family relationships of the inability of members to communicate verbally with each other must always be borne in mind. It is through stroke clubs that some families are able to begin to repair the damage and draw the strength to start afresh.

Approach to people with strokes

Let us imagine a typical example of a person suffering a stroke. He may have been ill or under some stress before but has been able to continue his normal life. Suddenly he sustains a stroke and when he comes round from his medical crisis he is changed.

Stroke is unique from the other illnesses described in this book because it produces such a sudden change in a person's functional state. "Stroke" is an apt word, for it must seem to the sufferer as if a thunderbolt or lightning flash has struck him. He comes round to a state of reasonable stability and finds that he has a paralysis of one side of his body. He cannot move his arm and leg; they feel heavy and alien to him. Sometimes he does not know where the arm and leg are. His mind is confused about what has happened and he searches for an explanation. Gradually as his mind clears he remembers that he fell down, or that a weakness suddenly overcame him.

If speech is affected and the perception of his surroundings is defective, then the effect is even more shattering. It may be difficult for him to control his bladder, and this is even more disturbing.

If rehabilitation is started, he can begin to feel that some recovery may take place and he begins to be hopeful that his present state is only temporary and full use of his body will come back again. Getting out of bed and sitting up in a chair, together with standing exercises, help him to feel the extent of the control of his body and the often long process of re-educating his function begins. Walking is a major problem which affects his morale and walking to the toilet, to the dinner table and to his favourite armchair become important events. He may need to be supported on his affected side as he walks. Feeding, dressing, washing and shaving take on a new significance when it is a question of whether the activity can be done independently or whether help is needed. It is in all these basic activities that he strives for independence, using the power and function of the unaffected side of his body to find new ways of performing these everyday tasks.

Often the person needs to be motivated to try to be independent. The feeling "if I wait, the movements will return" is common. But life must go on and we do not know for certain that movements, particularly in the affected arm, will return. It is when the condition persists over many months, and improvement is slow, that the sense of loss of function becomes great and often depression develops, together with a sense of doubt that life can really continue. Family, friends and work colleagues also become affected by the long drawn out progress of the illness and a gradual contraction of the sphere of social contacts often ensues.

It is at this point that the reality of the extent of the disability becomes apparent and changes have to be made by the family in their pattern of living. These changes have to take into account the residual disability of the person and the amount of care that he will need in the future. The social worker has a very important role to play in this process. She can help the family to make the adjustments to their lives which are necessary in their situation. She should understand how the disabled person feels and encourage him to take an active part within the family, to establish a new role for himself and to develop new interests. She can also help the family through the period of depression which can become extended if the adjustment is hard.

In later chapters ways are described whereby physical changes in the environment can help such families to cope with the problems of residual disability.

4 Diseases of the heart and lungs

In order to give a fairly brief account and simplified description of a few of the common problems which affect the clients we meet, it is necessary to realise that diseases of the heart may also have an effect upon breathing and diseases of the lungs also have an effect upon the heart.

In all forms of exercise, from climbing stairs to running a mile and from getting out of bed to doing the housework, the body requires oxygen which is taken in through the lungs. This is circulated in the blood which is pumped round the body by the heart. In the tissues oxygen is taken up and combines with nutritional substances to produce energy for doing work. Therefore diseases which affect any part of this process – that is, in lungs, heart or circulation – cause weakness and the inability to exercise without discomfort. The major discomforts which people feel are pain and breathlessness and these are the two symptoms which make people most anxious. Anxiety itself can have an effect on the amount of pain and breathlessness experienced.

Four major conditions are described below and these have been chosen from the many diseases of the heart and circulatory system and the respiratory system because they are those most frequently encountered by the social services worker.

Angina pectoris

Pain is the dominant feature of this condition and the pain is felt behind the breast bone and across the chest. It is often described as a constricting or crushing feeling. The amount of pain is usually in direct relationship to the amount of exertion and when it becomes very severe the pain radiates to the shoulder and down the left arm. Sometimes it might even extend to the neck and jaw. When the person stops activity and rests, the pain usually gradually passes away. It often comes on after meals and for this reason people sometimes think of it as indigestion. However, "indigestion" continuously felt in the chest rather than lower down should be referred to a doctor for investigation.

The pain in this condition is due to insufficient blood getting to the heart muscle itself, and this is called ischaemic heart disease (ischaemia means insufficient supply of blood). In Western civilisation the prevalence of ischaemic heart disease is high and gradually increasing, especially now in middle-aged, and even younger, men. There is an increasing incidence in women also. The causes are thought to be environmental and therefore should be able to be prevented. Lack of physical exercise, cigarette smoking, the eating of animal fats, obesity, high blood pressure and emotional stress are thought to be common causes of this disease.

Treatment is aimed firstly at controlling the pain by giving a drug, glyceryl trinitrate (TNT), in the form of small pills which can be placed under the tongue and allowed to dissolve slowly. People with angina are advised to carry the pills with them at all times and when exertion brings the pain on, to take a pill and rest. TNT should also be taken before exercise which is likely to produce pain, for example climbing stairs. The second form of treatment is to advise the person to adjust his way of life. This may mean giving up smoking, reducing weight and eating smaller meals slowly with a rest afterwards. A low-fat diet is considered beneficial. Doctors may advise the person to take up regular exercise which will help to reduce weight and increase the exercise tolerance. If the person is under emotional stress and anxiety, sedative drugs are often prescribed. Many people learn to live with this disease but in some clients it is seen to be crippling.

Heart attacks

Ischaemic heart disease can lead to coronary thrombosis or myocardial infarction, which is virtually the same thing. What happens is that the blood supply to the heart muscle is interrupted by a clot in the coronary artery. This lack of blood causes death of the heart muscle tissue and scarring which causes the heart gradually to lose efficiency. This condition is called myocardial infarction and can cause the heart to stop beating if not treated quickly.

Pain is felt in the same position as in angina, that is behind the breast bone and across the chest and is very severe and prolonged. It is not relieved by the taking of TNT pills or by rest.

Cardiac arrest

This means a cessation of heartbeat and most often occurs after myocardial infarction. Appropriate treatment should be given within five minutes, after which brain damage can occur and the person dies. Modern techniques of closed-chest cardiac massage and mouth-to-mouth artificial respiration have greatly improved the chances of recovery. Doctors, nurses, ambulance drivers and indeed many members of the public have had instruction in this vital form of first aid.

Treatment

After the initial crisis relief of pain, treatment for shock and rest in bed are the main forms of treatment, whilst attention is given to healing the damaged heart by various means. Coronary care units have been set up in many hospitals to provide specialised treatment for people following heart attacks. After the main crisis is over and treatment is underway the person is gradually got up and a graded course of activity begins.

Many people find that they are able to go home after about three weeks and, after a period of progressive rehabilitation, go back to a normal routine of activity, often returning to work after two to three months.

Sudden death occurs in about twenty-five per cent of people suffering a heart attack. In many cases this happens before medical help can be called. After the first forty-eight hours following an attack the death rate decreases rapidly, and it has been suggested that only one in ten people will die within a year, three in ten will live for up to five years and six in ten will live up to ten years. Long-term survival is probably more likely if the person changes his way of living, as described in relation to angina pectoris above.

Approach to people following heart attacks

Feelings of people who have had a heart attack are often a mixture of relief at having survived and anxiety and fear of another attack. A heart attack is often taken as a warning that life was becoming too stressful and the person is forced to review his lifestyle and to make changes which will help to avoid a recurrence. Now he knows that he will have to take life at a slower pace, worry less and relax more. Values may need to be changed also: for example, making do with less money rather than striving for more. This can be the turning point in a man's life, at which he learns to be happier with the things he already has, his relationships and his creative pleasures rather than constantly seeking the crock of gold at the end of the rainbow.

However, many people find this transition difficult for various reasons. More men than women suffer heart attacks and a man's lifestyle is often affected more drastically than that of a woman. A man's status, identity and role in society are based upon the job he does. If he is a teacher, an engineer or a builder, for instance, and has to change to a less taxing job, even if still in the same profession or trade, it may be seen as a failure and he feels that he loses status. Often a change of work will also affect him financially and it may be extremely hard for him to adjust his standard of living. When he loses his job or has to retire completely from work the blow can be great, and he is thrown back on his own internal resources.

An early retirement can bring the same problems as retiring at 65 and if there is no time for preparation, no building up of interests and other pursuits, then considerable losses are felt by the person and his family; loss of finance, loss of social role, loss of identity and loss of interest in life. Many people need help to adjust their lives and build up their confidence again. Introduction to new interests and encouragement to take up former pursuits are necessary to avoid the person deteriorating mentally and physically and placing strain upon family relationships. Help with finding work or changing jobs is given by Disablement Resettlement Officers in the Employment Services Agency.

Chronic bronchitis and emphysema

Chronic bronchitis is the name given to a disease which many people develop due to the long-continued action of various irritants upon the sensitive lining of the bronchial tubes. The irritants are commonly tobacco smoke, dust, smoke and fumes which may be occupational hazards or part of the general atmospheric pollution of towns. Chest infection may be an initial cause of the disease but usually only serves to aggravate the existing condition. Dampness, sudden changes in temperature and fog can cause a severe increase in the symptoms. This disease occurs mostly in middle-aged and elderly people and, as one would expect, in smokers rather than in non-smokers and in urban rather than rural dwellers.

The disease usually starts with repeated attacks of winter coughs which show a steady increase in severity and duration over the years until the cough is present all the year round. Gradual congestion of the bronchial tubes, which reduces the size of the air passages, produces difficulty in breathing and air becomes trapped in the base of the lungs with rupturing of the walls of the alveoli (the small sacs of the lungs where exchange of oxygen takes place between lungs and blood vessels). Other alveoli enlarge to compensate and the resulting lung damage is called emphysema. Chronic bronchitis and emphysema are so closely linked to each other in many individuals that the condition is often called "chronic obstructive airway disease".

Treatment

Irritation should be reduced to a minimum. The smoker should give up smoking and dusty and polluted atmospheres should be avoided if at all possible. This may entail a change of job although, at the age when this disease shows itself, that is often a difficult course of action to take.

Respiratory infection should always be treated promptly with antibiotics. Patients will produce large quantities of phlegm. They must be encouraged to cough it up and must be discouraged from taking cough suppressants and sedatives. Sleeping in a warm bedroom will often help to allay the discomfort of difficult breathing due to the cold atmosphere and, indeed, foggy, damp and windy weather is usually avoided as much as possible by sufferers.

Many people live for twenty to thirty years with this disease and often it remains static for long periods.

Approach to people with chronic bronchitis and emphysema

The most worrying symptom is difficulty in breathing, which can have a frightening effect. Every activity can become an effort; the more strenuous the activity the more breath is needed and therefore the symptoms become worse. Such activities as climbing stairs cause the person to gasp for breath and, if he then enters his cold bedroom and undresses for bed, by the time he lies down he is in a state of acute distress. Coughing follows and he has difficulty in getting to sleep. This is a common picture in elderly people and is often helped by bringing the bed downstairs and heating the bedroom. Some elderly people who are living alone sleep in their living rooms during the winter as, quite sensibly, they reason that having heated up one room all day, it seems silly to leave it for a cold bedroom at night. This is right, providing that they have a bed settee in that room on which to lie down and do not spend the night sitting up in an armchair, which leads to swollen legs and possible ulcers.

The social services worker will be concerned with the daily routine of the person with chronic bronchitis and emphysema and will be ready to offer advice which will help him to live with the minimum discomfort. Help with the more strenuous household tasks will avoid undue respiratory distress although he should be encouraged to remain as independent as possible and not restrict his normal social life. Help with heating the house will be an important consideration. The social services worker will also need to be aware of the dangers of respiratory infection and help the person to get speedy treatment from his doctor when required.

Bronchial asthma

Bronchial asthma is characterised by attacks of severe difficulty in breathing accompanied by wheezing, which is caused by temporary narrowing of the bronchial tubes due to muscle spasm and swelling of the mucous lining of the tubes. The resistance to airflow is therefore increased in the tubes.

Asthma can begin at any age but it usually starts in childhood or in middle age. The "early onset" asthma of childhood is usually due to an allergic reaction to substances contained in the air such as pollen, mite-containing house dust, feathers or animal fur. "Late onset" asthma in adults is usually not attributable to this kind of allergic reaction and the cause is so far unknown. In both types the symptoms are often aggravated by irritation caused by tobacco smoke, dust, acrid fumes and emotional stress. Strenuous exercise can provoke an attack, especially in children.

Asthma may take two forms. One is called episodic asthma, that is, the person experiences sudden violent attacks which can occur at any time. In between these the person is relatively free from symptoms. The difficulty in breathing during an attack is intense and takes the form of inability to breathe out. The person fixes himself with arms gripping furniture to hold the chest rigid and tries with all his effort to exhale. This becomes a conscious and exhausting effort. The attack may end abruptly within an hour or two, sometimes with prolonged coughing, but a wheezing sound may be heard in the person's breathing for many hours, or even days, afterwards.

Chronic asthma is the other type and the attacks are less conspicuous. The person may continually wheeze and be breathless on exertion. Coughing is frequent and recurrent respiratory infections are common.

Children suffering episodic attacks of an allergic nature usually have them in the summer when the pollen count is high, whilst adults suffering from chronic asthma find that it is worse during the cold winter months. Attacks look far more serious than they really are, for they are rarely fatal, but these spells of respiratory distress can be nevertheless very frightening to the individual.

Treatment

It is usually best for the sufferer to take up the position which he finds most comfortable during an attack. This is usually sitting up in bed or on a chair. Drugs are given in the form of inhalers from pressurised canisters.

Obviously if the asthma is caused by an allergic reaction, those substances which aggravate it should be avoided as far as possible. This is easier with an allergy due to animal fur, feathers or diet substances, than with one caused by a high pollen count in the air breathed. People who are allergic to dust should make sure that the bedroom is kept dust-free and it helps if the mattress also is vacuumed. A child should not be put in a lower bunk bed. If attacks are due to emotional

41

disturbance then sedatives may sometimes be given by the doctor.

Approach to asthmatic people

This can be an extremely crippling disease, especially when attacks are severe, and very frightening for the individual. The anxiety attached to this disease should be appreciated by the social worker and the person helped to adjust to his difficulties. He may need to be helped to avoid strenuous exercise, whilst continuing his normal life, and to deal with emotional stress as far as possible.

5 Diseases in old age

Imagine the human body wearing down after a lifetime of wear and tear. All tissues are ageing and losing the supple elasticity, flexibility and adaptability of youth. Physical and emotional stresses of life finally take their toll and certain diseases become common.

Circulatory diseases

Arteriosclerosis, or hardening of the arteries throughout the body, is widespread among elderly people. It is a progressive condition, no treatment is available and it is common to find more than one manifestation of its presence in a person. The arteries become inelastic, hard and "furred" up so that the quantity of blood which can pass through is reduced. This leads to ischaemia, which is the medical term used when any organ or tissue is not receiving sufficient blood for its needs. Profound or prolonged ischaemia will lead to death of the tissue, which is known as infarction or gangrene.

Ischaemia of the heart muscle is the underlying cause of angina, myocardial infarction and some forms of heart failure. It is due to narrowing of the coronary arteries.

Ischaemia of the legs caused by narrowing of the arteries to the legs, leads to painful ulcers (not varicose ulcers). In some cases gangrene can occur and then it is not uncommon for toes to shrivel and drop off; in extreme cases a foot may have to be removed by surgery. Another form is known as inter- mittent claudication and is a condition found in men who complain of pain in the calf of the leg whilst walking, so severe that they are forced to stop. The pain then passes off.

Ischaemia of the brain leads to many conditions, such as

stroke, arteriosclerotic dementia, Parkinson's-like gait and
mobility problems, blackouts and mental confusion.

The digestive system in old age

Diverticulosis is a condition in which pouches are found along
the large intestine. These are harmless unless they become
inflamed giving rise to pain on the left side of the abdomen,
fever and diarrhoea. When inflammation is present the condition is known as diverticulitis. Patients should be encouraged to take extra roughage, especially bran, which will help
to relieve the discomfort by producing a softer stool. It is
thought that a high-roughage diet also reduces the incidence
of inflammation.

Hiatus hernia The oesophagus or food pipe carries food
from the mouth down to the stomach. The stomach is in the
abdomen, which is separated from the thorax or chest by the
diaphragm, the main muscle of breathing. However, there is
a hole or hiatus in the diaphragm through which the oesophagus passes. In the condition of hiatus hernia, part of the
stomach protrudes upwards through this hole and is pinched
by the diaphragm. Heartburn is the predominant symptom.
It is often worse when lying down and can be relieved by
sitting up. It often comes on in the night and can cause some
elderly people to stay sitting up in a chair all night, which
can be detrimental to their health.

Constipation is a frequent complaint of older people. Many
people think a regular daily motion is essential to good health
and if they do not achieve this they complain of constipation.
Diet and exercise are the cornerstones of rational treatment.
People should be encouraged to increase roughage, fruit and
fluid intake and to move around. The use of drugs for relief
should be discouraged.

Diarrhoea most frequently is the result of aperients taken
for constipation, or as the side effect of other medicines, such
as antibiotics. Diarrhoea must be reported to the doctor if it
is a new symptom, as it may be associated with cancer of the
bowel.

Hypothermia

A normal, healthy person maintains his body temperature at
98.4°F, which is warmer than his surroundings, by a delicate
balance of heat production and heat loss under the control of

a "thermostat" in the brain, using various glandular products, especially thyroxine. Heat is made in muscles and the liver by breaking down food substances. It is lost through the breath, skin, sweat and urine. If more heat is lost than is produced the body will cool and a state of hypothermia will be present.

An old person is liable to become hypothermic if one or more of the following conditions arises:

(a) inadequate food intake;

(b) inadequate clothing;

(c) a very low living room or bedroom temperature;

(d) he is unable through physical or mental illness to take steps to keep himself warm and remedy any predisposing conditions – for instance, he cannot make up the fire;

(f) he has inadequate gland secretions, especially thyroid, to break down his food into heat;

(g) his "thermostat" has been put out of action by drugs, e.g. Largactyl.

A person who has a falling body temperature will appear apathetic and sluggish, paying little attention to his bodily needs, so that unless steps are taken to warm him he will get colder and colder. At very low levels the body cells can no longer function to make heat, the person will gradually cool down to room temperature and death will occur.

A cooling person will feel hard and cold, like marble, and the face is often puffy and swollen. First aid treatment should aim to prevent any further cooling, by any method that is available, while awaiting removal of the person to hospital.

Other conditions affecting the elderly

Infections are common in old people, partly due to a diminished resistance to germs and partly due to the prevalence of conditions predisposing to infection. *Pneumonia* frequently occurs in lungs already damaged by chronic bronchitis or heart failure. *Urine infection* occurs where the prostate gland (in men) is causing incomplete emptying of the bladder and where females have damaged bladders due to womb prolapse following difficult confinements. *Diabetics* are more prone to all infections and diabetes is common in later life.

Pressure sores are ulcers caused by interruption of the blood supply to the skin, resulting in death of the tissues. The area may blister, turn red, purple or black and eventually separate to leave a raw area of healthy tissue. Healing may take months and energetic measures should be taken to prevent such ulcers ever developing. Danger areas are where the bone is near the surface, i.e. at the hips, sacrum, heels, ankles and elbows. These areas must be protected from prolonged pressure by the use of foam pads, air mattresses, water beds, air rings and similar appliances.

Fractures and broken bones occur in the elderly as the bone structure changes and bones are more brittle. Minor accidents or stress on a bone may cause it to snap. Surgery is often needed to fix the broken pieces firmly together to allow healing to take place. A diet which is low in calcium and vitamin D will predispose to brittle bones.

Shingles is often very serious and painful in older people causing profound depression. It may also leave the person with persistent pain, known as post-herpetic neuralgia. Early treatment with modern remedies can cut short an attack and prevent neuralgia and so people should be advised to report to their doctor at once.

Glaucoma, a distressing, serious eye condition is commoner in old age. People with a painful red eye must be referred urgently to their doctor. Early treatment can save sight. Any person suffering loss of vision should be seen by an optician, who will usually prescribe spectacles but who can also refer more serious conditions to the doctor.

Cancer of all organs is commonly found. It is often slow-growing and is only discovered when widespread.

Danger signs in old people to be reported to the doctor

1. Shingles (see above).
2. Painful red eye (see "Glaucoma" above).
3. Sudden confusion in a person who is normally alert probably indicates the onset of an illness, e.g. pneumonia or heart failure. It may also be due to medicines being taken by the person.
4. Bleeding from anywhere.
5. Skin sores which do not heal – they may be a skin cancer.
6. Inability to pass urine, especially in elderly men.

6 Physical handicap in children

The main conditions which give rise to physical handicap in children are cerebral palsy, spina bifida with hydrocephalus and muscular dystrophy. Other important conditions are cardio-respiratory disorders, asthma, epilepsy, cystic fibrosis and juvenile rheumatoid arthritis (Still's disease). Haemophilia is also seen occasionally. These conditions are described briefly below together with an indication of current treatments (asthma and epilepsy have already been described in earlier chapters).

Cerebral palsy

This is a general term for a group of conditions characterised by disorders of movement and posture and following lesions in the brain which may have occurred before, during or after the birth of the child. Maternal rubella (German measles) during the first three months of pregnancy is one of the causes. Anoxia (lack of oxygen, especially to the brain) during and immediately after birth is the most common cause. The risk of cerebral palsy is increased by premature birth, abnormal position of the foetus and intracranial haemorrhage during and immediately following birth due to difficult delivery. Meningitis and encephalitis (both infections of the brain) in the infant are post-natal causes.

The ataxic (unco-ordinated) and athetoid (constantly moving) forms of cerebral palsy usually affect all four limbs and the body. The spastic forms may be limited to one side of the body (hemiplegia) or to the legs (paraplegia or diplegia), or may involve all the limbs (quadriplegia). In some forms of cerebral palsy there may be difficulty in chewing and swallowing and in speech (dysarthria and dysphasia). There may also

47

be fits, deafness, visual problems and intellectual impairment. There are many different conditions grouped under the term cerebral palsy and many variations within the same condition. However, the disability is mild in fifty per cent of all cases and only ten per cent are severely handicapped. Some degree of intellectual impairment is present in about sixty-six per cent of all cases (information from Elliott, *Clinical Neurology*, item 13 in the Bibliography).

Treatment

Fits are treated by medicines, hearing and sight problems are corrected when and if possible by the use of glasses and hearing aids and infections are always treated as quickly as possible. Otherwise, treatment involves the skills of the physiotherapist, occupational therapist and speech therapist in co-operation with the parents, in assisting the child's normal development as far as possible. Modern treatment is geared to the methods of Dr and Mrs Bobath in positioning the child to obtain the maximum functional use of his body and to minimise unwanted movements (spastic contractions and other involuntary movements).

Spina bifida and hydrocephalus

Spina bifida (meningomyelocele) is caused by defective development of the vertebrae in the lower part of the back, which is usually obvious at birth because the spinal cord has bulged through the gap and is marked by a dimple or sometimes an area of fatty tissue under the skin. There may be impairment of neurological function in the legs (paralysis) and the control of the bladder is often lost. Spina bifida is frequently associated with hydrocephalus, an abnormal enlargement of the skull due to defective drainage of cerebro-spinal fluid, and this causes pressure on the brain.

Treatment

Surgical treatment of spina bifida is usual within the first two days of birth, when repair is made to the spine to close up the gap. This must necessarily be done quickly to prevent infection. However, the child may be left with some paralysis in his legs and some urinary problems.

Hydrocephalus has more serious consequences for the child's subsequent functioning. It can be treated by the insertion of a valve into the head which drains excess fluid into a vein. However, most children affected by hydrocephalus would appear to have an associated malformation of some parts of the brain which causes muscular weakness in the arms and hands and an inability to co-ordinate movements. A squint may also be present. Perceptual problems may become apparent and the child appears to have difficulty in organising and making sense of the input from his senses. This affects the development of reading and writing, in particular.

Remedial treatment from physiotherapist and occupational therapist will therefore concentrate on helping the child to develop normal function and because of the range of difficulties, this treatment will continue throughout the child's school years.

Muscular dystrophy

The classification of the many diseases in this category is confusing. Some begin in childhood, others later in life. All are characterised by progressive weakness of groups of muscles, without disease in the central nervous system. The causes are unknown and there is no known cure.

The commonest and most severe form of muscular dystrophy in children is called Duchenne muscular dystrophy. It is genetically inherited through the female line and affects male children almost exclusively. The disease usually becomes apparent towards the end of the third year of life after walking has developed. The first noticeable symptom is clumsiness and difficulty in walking with frequent falls and particular difficulty in climbing stairs. With progressive weakness of the muscles of the hips, the child develops a waddling gait and he is unable to rise from the floor without using his hands to "climb up himself". Later, other groups of leg muscles become weak and the majority of these children are unable to walk by the time they are 10 years old. Weakness spreads to muscles in the arms and the body. Some children become very thin while others become obese. As the disease progresses the heart may become affected. Death usually occurs in the second decade of life from respiratory infection or heart failure.

Treatment

It is thought that regular physical exercise may delay the onset of contracture of the limbs and parents are taught passive exercises by the physiotherapist. Gradually supports are required for the child's body to prevent deformity and to keep the chest upright to facilitate breathing, and an electric wheelchair will be beneficial later to allow the child continued mobility. Independence should be retained in all activities for as long as possible and the increasing use of aids will facilitate daily life for both child and parents.

At school and at home children are encouraged to extend their experiences as much as possible in school work, in leisure pursuits and in social activities.

As with other physically handicapped children, it is of vital importance for the child with muscular dystrophy to be allowed to mature emotionally through independent choice and decision-making.

Cardio-respiratory disorders

The causes of abnormalities in the development of the heart of the foetus are largely unknown. Some defects, however, are due to maternal infections in the early weeks of pregnancy such as rubella.

Most of the abnormalities take the form of holes or gaps in the walls between the chambers and vessels of the heart. The effect is that the heart is unable to function efficiently because of seepage or "shunt" of blood from one side of the heart to the other when this should not happen, and consequently the heart has to pump harder in order to circulate the blood.

Nowadays, modern techniques in heart surgery usually ensure the repair of these defects in childhood and following successful operations life expectancy is normal. However, some defects are slow to show their presence and the child may be 10 years old before an operation can be performed. Some children, even after operation, may remain incapacitated to some extent. These children are often small for their age and have a reduced tolerance of exercise. The extent of their handicap will depend upon the way in which they and their parents react to the condition. Over-sheltering is natural but should be avoided and activities within the child's tolerance will not damage the heart further. Many "cardiac crip-

---

ples" with the right opportunities at school and at home are able to lead a full life and become "normal" adults.

Cystic fibrosis

This is a hereditary disease which affects the functioning of the pancreas. It is associated with an increase in the viscosity of the sputum which can lead to obstruction of the bronchial tubes and inflammation of the lungs. Pneumonia and lung abcesses are common complications. The child tends to sweat and to salivate profusely and appears under-nourished. Repeated attacks of respiratory infections are noticed in very young children and the stools are bulky and foul-smelling.

As the disease progresses, a cough becomes severe and wheezing is often present. There may be increased shortness of breath and the child is cyanosed (blue).

Treatment

The prognosis of this disease is much improved with modern treatments. Antibiotics combat infections in the lungs and the physiotherapist will show parents how to encourage drainage of the child's lungs regularly. Treatment for malfunction of the pancreas is usually conducted from a hospital clinic where long-term support is given to both the child and his parents.

Juvenile rheumatoid arthritis (Still's disease)

Rheumatoid arthritis in children often starts before the age of 5 and is accompanied by considerable systemic disorders which make the disease particularly unpleasant and the child particularly ill. As the child grows older the disease gradually merges into the form encountered in adults and described in an earlier chapter, but not until the child has spent long periods of time in hospital. Physical growth is often retarded. The treatment of Still's disease is similar to that given in cases of adult rheumatoid arthritis but is particularly concerned with the prevention of deformity. Education in hospital and at home may be necessary.

Haemophilia

Haemophilia is a hereditary disorder which is carried by the female line and affects the males. It is a disorder of blood coagulation characterised by a tendency to excessive bleeding and an inability of the blood to clot quickly. It is usually noticed in children within the first three years of life. Apart from danger of persistent bleeding from cuts, from tooth extraction and minor and major surgery (for other reasons), the main problem is bleeding into the joints, particularly the knees, ankles and elbows. When this happens there is pain and swelling in the joints and fever. There is a danger that when the blood does finally clot in the joint it may lead to a fusion (or ankylosis) of the joint with subsequent deformity. Anaemia may result if bleeding is profuse.

Treatment

There is no known cure for the disease. Splinting of joints may be required but should not be continued for too long in case fusion occurs. Drugs are given to reduce the pain and ice packs are also used for the same effect. Anaemia, if present, is treated with iron. Any surgery, however minor, has to be carefully planned and blood made ready for transfusion.

In order to limit the risks of bleeding into joints the child with haemophilia has to lead a somewhat sheltered and careful life avoiding trauma as much as possible. Some children who have a mild form of haemophilia are able to go to normal schools but children with a more severe form usually go to special schools.

Approach to children with physical handicaps

For every mother, before and when her child is born, there are expectations of its life. She will know or will be learning of the pattern of normal development, through all its stages, until the child is fully grown and becomes able to lead an independent life. To a certain extent all parents hope to live a better life through their children, hoping that they will achieve more than they themselves have done. "I want him to have everything that I never had."

When a child is born which is potentially handicapped in some way, it may be obvious from the first, as in spina bifida or in cerebral palsy, or the handicap may not become evident until the child begins to grow. Then the normal stages of development do not happen at the expected time and medical assessment may begin to show a pattern of malfunction which indicates a particular handicapping condition.

Whenever parents are told their child has a handicap, the

blow is great. Suddenly they no longer see the future of their child, and the normal expectations of its progress through life are dashed to pieces. It is at this stage that help must be made available, help to enable parents to question and understand the nature of their child's difficulties and to realise what they can do to help the child develop. Often there is a sense of panic, urgency and the need to give everything to the child and to protect it from itself and from the future.

In order to prevent the formation of an overwhelming concept of the "sick child" it is necessary for parents to give, but to allow the child to use what is given, in order to develop as an individual.

Parents of children with muscular dystrophy may not be told until the child is 3 or 4, when the disease makes itself known. This is a deteriorating disease and parents have to face the prospect of an early death. These children have become independent by this age and parents often, then, enable their child to have all the experiences he can, cramming activities into his life so that he can benefit to the full. They see an end to the child's life experience. However, parents whose child has been diagnosed as having spina bifida will learn that they have a disabled member of their family for life. This may be felt as an encumbrance upon the child and the family, a burden for life.

It is important that parents are told as much as possible about their child's disability and what can be expected in the future. At the same time, normal expectations need to be encouraged when there is hope that some development can be achieved.

Child development

The main consideration is that the parents should be totally involved in helping the development of their child as they would with an able-bodied child. When treatment is given by remedial therapists the parents should be present and taught at every stage of treatment how they can continue this at home. There may be problems of feeding, nappy changing, dressing and bathing and then it is important to help the mother to find easy ways of managing these activities and learning methods which will help her baby. These activities are usually problematic in conditions such as cerebral palsy, when the child may have abnormal spasm of muscles. Meth-

53

ods of positioning can be learned, to facilitate handling the child and help its physical development later on.

One needs to keep in mind the normal stages of development and enable the child to experience through each one of them, even though the pace of development may be slower and the child may need more help than an able-bodied child to benefit fully from each stage.

Awareness of self

At around 5 weeks of age the baby's eyes begin to focus and he makes visual contact with the world around him. He begins to use the expression of his face in response to others smiling and laughing at him. Then he begins to move his arms and legs more meaningfully and begins to explore his own body. Texture games are played, gripping and taking things to the mouth.

The physically handicapped child may not start to amuse himself in this way and needs to be helped to do so. The visually handicapped child needs extra stimulation to explore his world and his body through touch. If the child does not put his hand to his face then it can be put there for him.

Awareness of surroundings

After playing with his own body, peek-a-boo games are played, allowing the child to become aware of the people and things outside himself through use of sight, sound and touch. A variety of toys will help the able-bodied and disabled child to explore and begin to manipulate his environment. Particular toys may be indicated to help the disabled child and local toy libraries will often have available a number of toys which are useful. There are a growing number of toy libraries set up especially for physically and mentally handicapped children.

Rolling, sitting up and crawling

A handicapped baby may show an awareness of his surroundings as soon as any baby would but may be late in developing movement. By encouraging him to roll from side to side he will want to roll over on to his tummy and this will help to strengthen his back muscles ready for sitting up. Once he is ready to sit up then propping up in a position for play is indicated and therapists will advise on methods of helping his development. Crawling will depend on the amount of physical disablement present and patience is needed in constantly positioning the child to elicit movement.

At 6–8 months the child would be sitting up in a normal development and this posture allows the child to reach and balance as a preliminary to standing. It also enables him to explore more fully through play. Able-bodied children develop by being frustrated. To encourage a child to reach, a goody may be placed slightly out of reach so that he will want to move to gain the desired object. The more the child wants the object the more it fights to gain it.

Similarly, if the child is put in an uncomfortable position he has to move to make himself comfortable. This kind of approach can be used with a disabled child for it will induce the same motives – to be comfortable, to reach the desired object. If expectations are too low and the child is over-protected, he will not be motivated to develop.

Walking

Depending on the cause of the disability, walking and standing will be developments which require very expert training from the physiotherapist. These activities may be very late in development but should not hamper the child's learning if the means can be found for him to become mobile without the full use of his legs. This may involve the use of mobility toys which he can sit upon and propel himself.

Toilet training

Toilet training should be expected with the physically handicapped child unless there is an obvious medical reason for continuing incontinence. Some children have been continually put in nappies beyond the time when they could have been toilet trained.

Late development should not be expected as a matter of course. If treatment is given at an early stage the child may be brought up to date in his development. If left to develop at a very slow speed then he will be left further and further behind. When expectations of the parents drop then they may start doing more and more things for their child. He becomes a "handicapped child" and they become a handicapped family. For example, handicapped children are often not expected to sleep through the night. Why not? Maybe they have muscular spasms, but these can be reduced so that everyone gets a good night's rest. Again, the child cries often. Every parent learns the pattern of her child's crying and knows when and why he cries, and when to react and when to ignore it. It should be the same with the child with a handicap.

A child should always be given a method of communication if he cannot communicate normally, for this will allow him to develop relationships and language. Signals, gestures, pictures or other symbols may become a means to communication.

As the child gets older the family will often need the help of someone who understands the handicap in order to help with continuing physical development and the achievement of maximum independence. This help may come from a district handicap team or a hospital team of therapists.

Resort to numerous aids and equipment should usually be avoided, for these can develop the "disabled" image. Besides, too much physical support may prevent the child from developing independence. It is often better to take risks of the child falling than to support him too much, for then he will learn ways of moving independently and safely. Parents may be requesting aids when they really need to help the child find a different method of moving. Most remedial therapists prefer to try out equipment which would be purchased and used with able-bodied children, for example, from Mothercare, before recommending aids which are designed for disabled children, unless there is no other alternative.

Groups of parents meeting together with the common problem of a handicapped child can help to support each other through the early pre-school stages of their child's development.

Education

Parents are usually relieved when their child goes to school because with handicapped children this happens at the same age as with (or sometimes earlier than) able-bodied children. Special schools are highly developed to help children learn perceptually, emotionally, socially and academically and, if at all possible, children are moved to normal schools as soon as they can compete with able-bodied children. Sometimes the reverse happens and children with learning difficulties and obvious handicaps are brought into special schools either for a short time or on a permanent basis depending on their problems.

Special schools are usually graded into primary, middle and upper schools so that each child has the opportunity to experience the same progression of education as in normal schools. Special schools for children with handicaps employ, in addition to teaching staff, nurses and remedial staff (physiotherapists, occupational therapists and speech therapists) so that physical development can proceed alongside academic development. A wide range of activities – riding, camping, music, physical education, drama and so on – is offered to broaden the child's experience; in the upper school there is opportunity for academic achievement through examinations with the expectation that some children may be able to go on to further study and work.

Schooling may be interrupted if the sick child spends long periods of time in hospital, and teachers are available both in hospitals and for sick children at home.

If experience is delayed through slow learning it has been suggested that schooling should be extended for handicapped children beyond the age of 16.

Children at puberty and into adolescence begin to realise the implications of their disability for their future, in particular in the development of their individuality, sexual awareness and self-image. This can be a traumatic time and counselling at school related to sex education and the meaning of relationships is undertaken.

While their children are at school parents have the opportunity to meet together through parent/teacher groups. These groups can enable parents to share their experiences, learn from each other and gain mutual support in bringing up their children. Such groups are more easily formed through the schools than beforehand because parents have a common venue and common interest.

Residential schools can provide the opportunity for greater development towards independence for some children with physical handicaps.

From school to adult life

The transition from school to adult life is rarely easy for any young person and often presents considerable problems for young people with handicaps. Whereas the school has provided a varying routine with constant intellectual and social stimulation, the young person is then thrown back on the resources in the community for work and an adult routine of living. These resources can be extremely sparse, particularly when the young person cannot be as fully independently mobile in the wider environment.

The careers service becomes involved for the last two or three years of schooling to aid in the preparation of young people seeking vocational guidance and exploring the opportunities open to them after leaving school. There are also residential assessment centres where physically handicapped school leavers can go to be assessed for further education and work. However, it can be a hard and soul-destroying time for the school leaver, who has often to fight to become accepted as an equal member of society with able-bodied folk.

Those young people who have had the greatest opportunity, both at home and at school, to develop their skills, individuality and drive and who have matured emotionally often manage to integrate fully into the able-bodied world. But many others are left behind and can never compete. The most important requirement for these young adults is that they continue to experience a full life, and are enabled to mature fully. This means a varied routine of work (albeit in sheltered employment or at an occupation centre), and the opportunity to expand socially and to make meaningful relationships with their peers. Many additional resources are required in the community to enable these aims to be achieved. A great deal more needs to be done for this age group.

PART TWO

Physical handicap and society

7 The social consequences of disability

There are over a million physically handicapped people in Britain: that is, around one person in every fifty has some severe and incurable ailment that prevents the carrying out of activities the rest of us take for granted. Some cannot walk, or talk, or even get out of bed on their own. Many more can walk, but only for a few paces, and that with difficulty. Others have lost the use of their hands, or can use them only with pain. Yet others with heart and lung disorders may appear quite well, but are soon exhausted and cannot do much for themselves. People with these handicaps find it difficult or impossible to go about their daily business, and in consequence find that their relationships with other people are affected as well.

Integrating the Disabled – the Snowdon Report published by the National Fund for Research into Crippling Diseases in 1977 – recommended a major effort towards integration by schools, hospitals and local authorities. The recommendations of the report were accepted by some organisations at once, and interest in integrating disabled people more fully into society continues to grow. There have been great advances in the understanding and help given to disabled people during the last decade, yet despite all the improvements, the handicapped are still socially disadvantaged and still misunderstood by other people.

The practical difficulties of getting about do much to divide the disabled from the rest of society. Despite the recommendations of the Chronically Sick and Disabled Persons Act, many public buildings are still inaccessible to people in wheelchairs. Libraries, adult education centres, community centres and swimming pools may have entrances that defy all attempts to admit a wheelchair and may present obstacles to people with walking difficulties. Other places, such as post offices, small shops, and ordinary houses are even worse, for as well as difficulties of access, they may also be so small that there is no room to turn the chair around if one manages to get in in the first place. In other words, disabled people find it very hard to go to clubs, attend meetings and classes, shop, borrow books or even visit their friends. The world was built for the able-bodied and disabled are often excluded from everyday affairs.

Problems of employment and income also set the disabled apart from their able-bodied counterparts. There are very few jobs of work that the severely disabled can do, and even the mildly disabled find themselves at the bottom of the list for jobs while there is unemployment in the country as a whole. Although state benefits do ensure against destitution, they provide a less easy lifestyle than that of the average wage-earner. Disability is in itself a source of much expense. Clothes wear out faster on people who have to wear calipers or use crutches and other appliances. Do-it-yourself jobs and home-made food and clothes are not easy to accomplish when one's limbs are impaired. In spite of welfare benefits, most disabled people are poor people, and this too helps to set them apart from the rest.

Unemployment is a problem not only for its effect on the family finances but also for its effect upon the morale and the social position of the disabled person. Our self-esteem is much tied up with our ability to support ourselves and our place in society is usually derived from what we do for a living. The unemployed tend to be seen as ne'er-do-wells or unfortunates who are not quite as good as everybody else. The disabled often feel that other people stigmatise them in this way even when their unemployment is unintentional.

Nowadays we do not see our jobs just as a means of earning a living, we expect them to be vehicles for testing and satis-fying our abilities and our ambitions as well. Few people would accept the view that work is just a necessary evil done to keep starvation at bay. Yet to many disabled, work, if they have any at all, is just such a drudgery. Disabled people tend to be given the most boring of jobs, for no one else will do them. Those who can only work sitting down find themselves doing the dullest of work sorting and checking the work of others more skilled than themselves. Many people become infirm towards the end of their working lives and have to give up responsible and challenging posts and accept routine clerical work instead. Skilled workers such as drivers, technicians and craftsmen can find themselves sorting nuts and bolts or sweeping the floor.

For the disabled school-leaver, lack of a suitable job may be the one thing that marks him out from among his able-bodied contemporaries. Where other youngsters have a choice of jobs, including those which offer training in some skill, the disabled young person has much less choice and may never find work at all. Lack of workmates can mean lack of any mates, for most young people make friends among those they work with. As most handicapped children have to travel to school, leaving school means leaving friends behind, and the handicapped school leaver may find himself or herself suddenly friendless.

Recreational activities are valued both for themselves and for the opportunity they give to meet people and to make new friends. Difficulties of access make it hard for the disabled to join in the work of clubs and societies. Lack of friends and lack of interests reinforce each other, for we make friends through our interests, and we also pursue new interests in the company of friends. Disabled people can soon find that they have very few of either.

Thus, the presence of a handicapping condition can in itself cut off the disabled person from the company of other people. However, even when the problems of mobility and access have been dealt with, another barrier to social integration has to be overcome and that is the attitude of other people towards the disabled. People react towards the handicapped the same way that they react to any other group noticeably different from themselves: they reject them.

Many people who are basically quite kindly cannot bring themselves voluntarily to approach a noticeably handicapped person. On meeting such a person they become very embarrassed, and awkward in speech and manner. They avoid looking the other person in the eye, and seem unable to talk normally for fear of saying the wrong thing. Some get round the problem by talking to the disabled person's companion instead – hence the oft-quoted faux-pas "Does he take sugar?" Others solve it by putting the handicapped person into a role they already know how to deal with: that is, they treat him as a child, and gush at him or talk down to him. Some able-bodied people freely admit that the sight of a handicapped person "gives them a turn". This feeling of discomfort shows itself in more important ways than just occasional embarrassed meetings. A genuine reluctance on the part of some of the able-bodied to have to see handicapped people around them every day leads to severe social difficulties for anyone unfortunate enough to possess a visible impairment. Employers may refuse to appoint a disabled person to a vacancy he or she is quite capable of filling, and in a building with no access problems. Many businesses and public services employ no disabled whatsoever. Some of this reluctance to employ may come from a conviction that the disabled cannot pull their weight, but it is just as likely to arise from a general feeling of embarrassment in the presence of a disabled person.

It is the practice in Britain to send handicapped children to special schools which cater for the specific disability. There may be good educational reasons for this specialisation, but one undoubted side effect is to reinforce the idea in people's minds that these children belong to a different category from everybody else. Able-bodied children do not get the chance to mix with them and they tend to shy away when they come in contact with them.

People continue to shy away right into adult life, and this avoidance has bad social consequences for the disabled adult. People feel reluctant to chat to a handicapped neighbour. Shopkeepers can be seen and heard to feel embarrassed when serving a disabled person, and that particular person may in turn feel reluctant to return to that particular shop. Even when all the barriers to access and mobility have been removed, social activities can be made difficult because of the obvious reluctance of the able-bodied to associate with those who are disabled.

This disinclination to associate with the handicapped has in the past led to large and expensive projects specifically designed to segregate the handicapped from everyone else. The Victorian philanthropists' answer to any social problem was to build an institution in which to house it, and so we have, to this day, massive red-brick buildings to house the mentally handicapped, the mentally ill, the ordinarily sick, the orphans, the delinquent and the blind. As the field of philanthropy expanded, so did the total mass of institutional building, and so we have special homes, hostels, workshops and schools for those handicapped people who lack the physical ability or the mental determination to cope on their own.

Many people who should know better still express the view that disabled people are better off among their own kind, forgetting that the only thing they may have in common with other handicapped people is some physical impairment. Often years of incarceration in some institution have destroyed the handicapped person's ability to care for himself, and to mix with other people who are not from the same institution. People working in such places can often be heard to say that their patients could not cope on their own, or that they exhibit some socially undesirable character trait that would make them unacceptable outside, forgetting as they do so that it is the institution that has made them like that. To a lesser extent, the same happens to persons whose sole opportunity to mix with other people is via some club or day centre. They cease to see that there can be any form of lifestyle outside of it. Care in the community can mean being institutionalised but going home to sleep.

The handicapped adult who wishes to become independent of his or her family has more than just physical difficulties to overcome. He may have to break out of the care situation, and overcome any attitudes in himself that are more appropriate to the institution than to the outside world. He has also to stay afloat in a society in which almost everything, physical, mental and social, has been designed with able-bodied persons in mind, and in which it is assumed that the disabled person does not wish to take part. He will often meet with embarrassment and discouragement when he tries to do those things that everyone else takes for granted. If people are hostile, they will ignore and discourage him; if they are friendly they may try to over-protect him. Not surprisingly, some disabled people react to this in ways that do not help to further their integration into society. If they react by losing their tempers they are accused of being ungrateful, or of having a chip on their shoulders. If they play up to the stereotype of helplessness – as the easiest way out – they find that they have confirmed people's opinions of them as helpless and dependent. It takes a very sane, sensible and well-adjusted person to cope with other people's misconceptions all the time; to put his own views forward firmly, but without aggression; and to thank people for their offers of help, but to go quietly on with his or her own method of doing things.

Having outlined the main social disadvantages of being disabled, it is only fair to say that there have been some great improvements in society's attitudes to disabled people during the last decade. The Chronically Sick and Disabled Persons Act of 1970 has made it the duty of all local authorities to provide services for the disabled, and of all public bodies to ensure access for wheelchairs and people with walking difficulties in any building into which the general public are entitled to go. The institution of the Attendance Allowance, the Invalid Care Allowance and the Mobility Allowance has done much to make financial matters easier for the disabled, ill and infirm. The institution of the Mobility Allowance illustrates perhaps more clearly than anything else society's attitude that the disabled are expected to go out and about. Pressure groups such as the Disabled Drivers' Association and the Disablement Income Group keep before the public eye the image of a body of people who, despite physical impairment, expect to enjoy the same social rights as everybody else and who are obviously as intelligent as anybody else when it comes to discussing them.

The attitude of some of the voluntary bodies is beginning to change. Homes and hospitals are starting to allow more personal freedom (though many still allow no visitors in bedrooms and have official bedtime and lights-out). Some schools for disabled children now expect the youngsters to want to live away from their parents when they grow up, and they help to prepare them for independence, work and marriage. There are even a small number of married persons' flatlets being built in housing complexes for the disabled (though, as any sort of purpose-built housing is in extremely short supply, young couples may have to wait a long time before being given one).

There is still a great deal of room for improvement in the way other people treat those about them who are physically impaired, and it is part of the duty of the caring professions to help other people achieve better understanding of the disabled. Nurses, doctors, care staff, social workers and therapists can do a great deal to help, if they set a good example to others by treating the disabled as though they were normally intelligent adults. The handicapped themselves can do a lot to educate the public, simply by being around in society often enough for people to get used to the idea. Those who do manage to find work will find that most other people will get used to them in time and will eventually come to accept them as equals, if only they can keep their patience and their wits about them in the early days of their acquaintance.

Those involved in helping the disabled can do a great deal to help during this difficult period by supporting and encouraging the handicapped person as he tries to fit into this new situation. It is not enough to provide the wheelchair and the ramp, one must help the recipient of these aids to cope with the world outside the home and the people he will meet in it. It helps, perhaps, if one explains that most people are not really hostile but instead rather shy and embarrassed to be meeting someone with a disability they have not met with before. The able-bodied are afraid of offending and embarrassing the disabled person by looking at him or saying the wrong thing and it is really up to the disabled person (who ought to be used to it by now) to put them at their ease by talking to them as though they were acting normally. As one chairbound lady was heard to say, "Disabled people have to be like royalty. They have to be good at putting people at their ease." If the handicapped and those who work with them can bear these points in mind, especially when the general public are being at their most irritating, then the barriers will become broken down and disabled people will have made the public aware of their needs and potentialities.

8 Acts of Parliament affecting the rights of disabled people

The rights of disabled people are laid down in the following acts of Parliament. Local authority and national government departments have a duty to see that the terms of these acts are carried out properly. A study of the acts makes very interesting reading, especially if taken in chronological order, for they illustrate the attitudes to disability prevalent at the time they were drafted and show how ideas have changed over the last thirty years.

The Local Authority Social Services Act 1970

This act of Parliament brought into being the new social services departments that had been recommended by the Seebohm Report. The personal social service provisions hitherto divided between the old children's departments, health and welfare departments and mental health departments were brought together into one comprehensive social service which aimed to provide help for all people and families in trouble.

Under the terms of this act, the new departments became responsible for carrying out the duties of local authorities to handicapped and infirm people as laid down in the National Assistance Act and the Chronically Sick and Disabled Persons Act.

The National Assistance Act 1948

This act was designed to replace the old Poor Law which gave an out-dated and punitive form of poverty relief. It was made to complement the National Insurance Acts of 1946, in providing financial assistance to people in need so that no-one need fall below a certain level deemed necessary to sustain life and promote reasonable standards of living. As the financial benefits conveyed to the disabled by these acts have been considerably changed in recent years it is unnecessary to describe them here. The main advantage the National Assistance Act gave to the disabled was in Part III of the Act, wherein local authorities were empowered to provide many services designed to improve the quality of their lives.

Local authorities were given the duty of providing homes and hostels for elderly and disabled persons who were unable to care for themselves and who had no-one to look after them. The term "Part III Accommodation" refers to the old people's homes set up in response to Part III of the Act. They replaced the old workhouses, which had a rather punitive atmosphere and austere surroundings; though, as some of the new homes had to make do with old workhouse buildings for some years, it is probable that some of the residents did not notice much of a difference. (One of us clearly remembers the transformation of the "Grannies' room" at the local institution when the wooden benches were thrown out and replaced by upholstered armchairs, and the room received its first carpet.) Local authorities could use the facilities of another local authority or charitable body, and pay the appropriate fee. They were also empowered to charge residents according to their means, though they had to leave them part of their pension for personal expenses.

The Act also made it the duty of local authorities to inspect and to register private residential establishments for the elderly and disabled. They were empowered to enforce minimum standards of health and safety provision and staffing and equipment.

The National Assistance Act, in Section 29, gave to local authorities the power to promote the welfare of all handicapped persons, i.e. blind, deaf, dumb and disabled, ordinarily resident in the area of that local authority. It did not, however, oblige them to do so. The recommendations were as follows. The local authority should compile and maintain classified registers of persons in need of assistance, such as blind, deaf and crippled, and should take steps to inform people on these registers of the services available to them from local and other sources. Local authorities were also given the power to provide workshops, home-worker schemes and tuition in handicrafts for disabled people unable to work in open employment. They were enabled, too, to provide instruction

69

in methods of overcoming disability either in the home or in classes, and this was often interpreted as providing craft instruction for infirm and disabled people, and braille tuition for the blind.

The extent to which local authorities used their powers under this act varied greatly, and indeed still does. Fortunately for the disabled, the Chronically Sick and Disabled Persons Act 1970 was a lot more specific in its requirements.

The Chronically Sick and Disabled Persons Act 1970

This act made further provision for the welfare of disabled people. Its recommendations were made in stronger terms than those of the National Assistance Act. Local authorities now had a positive duty to provide amenities and services recommended under the older act, and legislation for access was made for the first time in this country.

By the time the Act was passed, disabled people themselves were beginning to make their opinions felt through pressure groups such as the Disablement Income Group, and the general public were becoming aware that the disabled saw themselves as normal people whose place was out in society rather than tucked away in some institution. The Chronically Sick and Disabled Persons Act reflected this view, for it gave local authorities direct instructions for making it easier for disabled people to get around.

Under the terms of the Act it is now the duty of local authorities to find out how many people living in their areas are deaf, blind, physically handicapped and mentally handicapped. They also have the duty of ensuring that these handicapped people are informed about all the services available to them, including those from outside sources such as charities and trust funds. Most local authorities carried out this duty by conducting a household survey to find out how many disabled people lived in their area, very soon after the Act became law. Though useful as a planning exercise, such surveys do not really tell the local authority the identity of handicapped persons, for the surveys were usually done in the years immediately following the Act, and they are too expensive to repeat at frequent intervals. As most of the disabled, blind and deaf are elderly, many of those originally seen will be dead, and replaced by newer elderly disabled people. Some local authorities could only afford a sample survey, such as one in four households, and thus their results could only be used for estimating the need for services and not for identifying disabled persons. In order to keep to the terms of the Act, local authorities should now be advertising their services to disabled people so that anyone in need of them will be encouraged to come forward and apply.

The Act made it the firm duty of the new social services departments to carry out the recommendations for the care and rehabilitation of all handicapped people, and mentioned in particular home help, meals on wheels, aids to daily living, adaptations to the home, telephone, occupation in the home, occupation centres and outings, provided only that in the opinion of the local authority the person concerned was in need of these services. The Act also specifically mentioned a duty to provide or assist with the provision of transport of disabled people to places of occupation, entertainment and education. Shortages of cash have made it difficult for some local authorities to provide these services. Different criteria for interpreting the Act have given rise to wide variations in the way services are given in different local authorities and a patient moving from one area to another can find himself not eligible for services he used to receive before he moved.

Part Three of this act makes it the duty of local housing authorities to make provision for the handicapped and infirm, though these requirements are gone into more thoroughly in the Housing Acts, which will be dealt with later. Special housing takes time to plan and to build and like all housing is very expensive. Because of this, many local authorities have not yet made provision for housing all the disabled who require it.

Perhaps the greatest advance made by this act was the requirement that all public buildings should be made accessible to disabled people. All persons and organisations owning buildings to which the general public have access must now make sure that people in wheelchairs and with walking difficulties can get into those buildings. They must also make toilet and car park facilities accessible. Local councils responsible for the erection and maintenance of public toilets must provide at least one cubicle into which a wheelchair can be taken. Hotels, restaurants and theatres must also provide toilet facilities for the disabled. Schools, colleges and universities are specifically mentioned in the Act, and they must now have free access for wheelchair users and suitable toilets and parking space. The access requirements laid down in this act show very clearly that the government of the day saw the disabled as having the same rights to partake in social activities as everybody else, and having the same need for education, entertainment and social responsibility as well.

The Act made it clear that disabled people should have some say in their own affairs. Local and national government advisory committees such as those dealing with war pensions, housing, national insurance, industrial injuries and youth employment must have on them at least one person familiar with the problems of disabled people, and that person must be a disabled person whenever a suitable one can be found.

Section 17 of the Act made recommendations for the care of disabled people in hospitals. The regional hospital boards were to ensure that the young chronic sick and disabled were not accommodated in geriatric wards as they had often been in the past. Problems of accommodating people in need of care will be dealt with in more detail in the chapter on residential accommodation.

The Act also introduced the disabled car badge scheme under which disabled drivers and passengers could park more freely than other road users.

The Chronically Sick and Disabled Persons (Amendment) Act 1976

This very short act of Parliament added to the earlier Act the requirement that all new business premises should be built with access and facilities for the disabled. The Act was passed to make it easier for handicapped people to go to work in offices, shops, factories and railway premises. It also made it more difficult for employers trying to evade their responsibilities under the Disabled Persons Employment Acts, for now they would not have the excuse of inaccessible buildings to put forward.

The Disabled Persons (Employment) Acts 1944 and 1958

Most of the legislation affecting the employment of disabled people comes from these acts, which make it very clear that the governments of the day acknowledged the rights of disabled people not only to work, but also to have special facilities for training and for finding employment.

The 1966 Act defined the disabled person as follows:

"A person who, on account of injury, disease or congenital deformity, is substantially handicapped in obtaining or keeping employment, or in undertaking work on his own account, of a kind which apart from that injury, disease or deformity would be suited to his age, experience and qualifications."

Both physical and mental disabilities are included in this definition, and the later Act further defined the disability as being likely to be of twelve months' duration or more.

Under the terms of the Acts the Secretary of State for Employment must maintain a register of disabled people who are capable of working and who are looking for work. Disabled persons may apply for registration at their local Employment Service Agency or careers office, and will be provided with a certificate, the "green card", which they can show to their employers or prospective employers. If the disabled person's handicap is not a visible one, he or she may be asked to produce medical evidence before being registered. Registration is not compulsory, and disabled people who do register may apply to have their names removed from the register at a later date if they so wish. Registration for employment purposes is not the same as registration for social services and a disabled person may elect to register for either, both or none at all. Some disabled people, particularly those with a minimal, or invisible, handicap feel that having to answer "Yes" to the question "Are you a registered disabled person?" reduces their chances of finding employment. However, there are several distinct advantages to being registered, for only those so designated may be taken on under the quota system, given designated jobs and enrolled in special training and employment schemes.

The Act enabled the government to set up various rehabilitation and training schemes for the disabled, and also empowered the Department of Employment to pay for training at other recognised establishments.

All local employment offices (now called Jobcentres and Employment Service Agencies) were expected to employ a Disablement Resettlement Officer to advise disabled people seeking employment, and to liaise with other agencies in providing rehabilitation, retraining and employment.

The 1944 Act laid down the requirement that all commercial enterprises and local authorities employing more than twenty full-time workers, or their equivalent in part-timers, must employ a workforce three per cent of which must be registered disabled people. Employers were instructed to keep records of the disabled in their employ, and to submit this information to the appropriate government department when required. Failure to employ the required number of disabled people is not in itself an offence (presumably, the rights of existing employees had to be protected) but employers with less than the quota commit an offence if they dismiss a disabled person, or if they recruit further able-bodied staff. All employers were allowed by the Act to be given a permit to recruit further able-bodied staff even though below the quota if they could prove that the vacancies were unsuitable for disabled people or if no suitable disabled persons had applied for them. The Act lays down penalties of fines and eventual imprisonment for offences against its terms; however, employers are very seldom prosecuted, and it is generally agreed that some organisations do not take this legislation seriously.

The 1944 Act made it possible for the government to designate certain forms of employment as being for disabled persons only. To date, only the jobs of car park attendant and passenger lift attendant have been so designated. Employers may apply for a permit to engage able-bodied people for these jobs in the same way as they may do so under the quota scheme. Many disabled persons' pressure groups, and the authors of the Snowdon Report referred to in Chapter 7, have expressed the view that designated employment as it is now does little to enhance job opportunities for disabled people, and may even give outsiders the idea that such jobs are all that the disabled are capable of doing.

The 1944 Act enabled local authorities to set up or subscribe to sheltered workshops and home worker schemes for disabled people unable to work in open employment because of slow working speed, irregular attendance or need to be absent frequently for medical treatment. The 1958 Act made it a positive duty of local authorities to provide this service, and also enabled local authorities to be helped to finance these schemes from central government funds.

The Housing Act 1974

The passing of the Housing Act made it possible for local authority housing departments to give grants for the repair and improvement of sound, privately owned houses built before 1961.

There are various ways in which a householder or landlord of a private house may benefit under this act, and the amount of financial help available varies from one-half of the costs to up to ninety per cent if the house is in a housing action area. The disabled benefit from the provision of this act alongside everybody else, but in addition improvement grants may be payable for any work required to make a dwelling suitable for a disabled resident, even if the work done would not otherwise be eligible for grant-aid.

Local authorities must give a grant to any householder not having standard amenities such as sink, bath, toilet and running hot and cold water, who wishes to install them (provided that the house is otherwise in fit condition and likely to last at least fifteen years). The local authority is also empowered to grant aid for the installation of additional fittings of this type, if a disabled person is unable to make use of existing fittings. For example, a house could already have one or more bathrooms upstairs, but if the disabled person because of his disability could not get up the stairs an additional bathroom could be installed on the ground floor.

The Housing Rents and Subsidies Act 1975

This act reflected the view then prevailing that good housing standards for people with low income could best be improved by subsidising the tenant rather than subsidising the house. For the first time, people in privately rented houses and flats could have some help towards paying the rent. As the private rented sector contains many of the most deprived families, this act did a great deal towards giving help with the cost of housing to those who needed it most. The disabled, because they are often living on low incomes, benefited by the general terms of the Act, but also received special concessions of their own.

The Act enabled tenants of council houses and new town houses to be given a reduction in rent if their income fell below a certain prescribed level. Disabled people are given a larger rebate than other people. Such concessions are, of course, means tested, and are not given to people who are receiving supplementary benefit, for that already includes a sum towards paying the rent. Tenants of private landlords (including housing associations) who have very low incomes and are not receiving supplementary benefit can receive a rent allowance from their local authority. Disabled people are given higher levels of rent allowance than other people.

The Act also obliged local authorities to make rate rebates to people or families whose incomes were very low. Disabled people registered with the local authority are given a larger rebate than usual. Disabled occupants of houses which have had to be extended or adapted to meet their needs can claim exemption from paying rates on the improvement, even if it would otherwise increase the rateable value of the house.

People who are receiving supplementary benefit are not eligible for rate rebates as well and it is necessary to consider carefully which benefit would most help the person concerned. Often the client is better off receiving supplementary benefit because of all the other benefits such as free prescriptions, dental treatment, school meals and so forth that go with it. A disabled person unsure of which to claim should be advised to ask to see a visiting officer from the Supplementary Benefits Commission.

The Rating (Disabled Persons) Act 1978

This amended parts of the General Rate Act of 1967 and the equivalent parts of the Scottish rating legislation, and gave greater provision for rate rebates for disabled people. Where a property includes a room used predominantly by a disabled person, or has amenities to meet his needs, then the rates paid by the householder will be reduced.

Fixed amounts are deducted from the rate bill for a room, bathroom or lavatory used mainly by a disabled person, for floor space needed to manipulate a wheelchair and also for a garage, car port or parking bay used mainly by the handicapped person. Variable amounts, as assessed by the local authority, can be deducted from the rates paid, for heating installation, lift, covered way between house and garage or for garage and car space where the disabled person shares this with other people. The assessment can be appealed against in the county court.

Either the disabled person himself or another member of the household can apply for the rebate, according to whoever normally pays the rates.

9 The role of the helping professions

In order to give the best service to the handicapped person, members of the different professions involved in helping him need to work very closely together. The National Health Service, the local authority social services and the voluntary bodies can all do a great deal to help the handicapped person to lead a meaningful life, and if individual staff co-operate with one another they will both increase their professional knowledge and make a worthwhile contribution at the same time. Sometimes a problem which seems insuperable to one worker can be solved or at least alleviated by the knowledge and experience of a member of another profession. It is useful therefore, for all workers with handicapped people to have some idea of what members of other professions have to offer.

Social services staff

The social worker

Social workers are employed very largely by local authority social services departments and work either in social work area teams, or attached to a hospital. A few are employed by charities. Most social workers nowadays are trained, and their education consists either of a degree in the social sciences followed by a year's special training in social work methods, or a two-year course in social work. Both types of course lead to the Certificate of Qualification in Social Work, and both require at least a year's practical work in the field prior to admission.

Social workers act as a link with other professions and also as the client's link with special services and with the community. Though much of their time, in area social services teams at least, has to be spent in helping problem families and children in trouble with the law or at risk from neglect, they do have specific duties towards handicapped people as well.

The social worker goes into the home to assess the amount of help needed from the social services and takes into account both needs of the client and the help already available to him from family friends and neighbours. He or she is then in a position to recommend such services as home help, meals on wheels and aids to independence. The social worker should also be able to call in help from other workers such as occupational therapists, craft instructors and family aides. Often the social worker takes part in the joint assessment of need alongside the doctors, nurses and hospital therapists, especially when the patient is about to be discharged from hospital.

The social worker is also trained to assess the emotional atmosphere surrounding the client and his family, and to help them to come to terms with the difficulties of disabled living and the inevitable strains this places on both relatives and friends. The hospital social worker is especially valued for her skill at dealing with loss and is often called in to help families and patient to prepare for approaching death. The social worker's skills can also be used to help the patient come to terms with disability and to learn to live with distressing complaints such as disfigurement, incontinence and epilepsy. (Other professions also fulfil this role of intelligent listener and nurses, therapists and care staff can do a lot of good if they can find the time to listen when the patient needs to say something. Though the social worker should be called in for the more severe cases of need it is extremely inhumane to stop a patient in distress by telling him to keep his problems for the social worker to hear.)

Social workers need to have a good knowledge of financial benefits available to the disabled as many problems can be solved just by putting a bit of money into the situation (e.g. for taxi rides, babysitters, dress alterations and kitchen gadgets).

The occupational therapist

Most local authorities now employ at least one qualified occupational therapist to act as adviser on aids and adaptations for the disabled and to undertake rehabilitation programmes in the home. Good local authorities now have at least one in every area team, or an equivalent number working from a central base, and may also provide them with aides who are trained on the job to take over some of the less demanding work. Occupational therapy technicians also assist by making and adapting aids, and by installing simple adaptations in the home at the recommendation of the occupational therapists.

The occupational therapist in the local authority visits clients at home and assesses their capabilities and their need for services. Sometimes this is done jointly with a social worker but, in any case, the occupational therapist is available to advise and assist social workers dealing with disabled people. Occupational therapists also plan rehabilitation programmes and devise diversionary activities in conjunction with domiciliary handicraft instructors. They work very closely too with home helps, residential and day centre staff and others who are helping to keep the client independent and out in the community.

Occupational therapists must all be state registered and this is achieved upon gaining the Diploma of the British Association of Occupational Therapists or overseas equivalent. Students, who must be over 18 and possess five "O" Levels and one "A" Level, take a three-year course which includes theoretical studies in anatomy, physiology and psychology in addition to practical placements in hospitals for both physically and mentally ill people. In social services departments they are especially valued for their knowledge of disabling diseases and their understanding of hospital procedures and practices. More information on the work of occupational therapists is given later in the chapter where their role in hospitals will be discussed.

Residential care staff

The staff of residential homes for children, disabled adults and elderly persons come from a variety of professional backgrounds. There is no one form of training recognised as qualifying a person for this type of work. Many hold no formal qualifications at all though experience makes them skilled and valuable workers. Quite a number are qualified as nurses, others as residential social workers, one or two hold qualifications in institutional management and a few hold the new qualification, the Certificate of Social Service (CSS). Residential child care staff are quite often qualified schoolteachers. The vast majority have no formal qualifications simply because there is very little opportunity to acquire them. College places in residential social work studies are few and far between. The CSS has not had time to get properly off the ground yet, though it has great potential. Despite this lack of formal training some staff are making a real contribution towards the development of residential care as a helping profession.

Residential staff are responsible for the domestic organisation of the home and the material and social welfare of the residents. They perform basic care duties such as washing, dressing and feeding those who cannot do this for themselves, and they endeavour to promote meaningful occupations such as crafts, hobbies, outings and social events. They often take part in rehabilitation programmes and sometimes devise their own, it not being uncommon for an elderly short-stay patient to come into a home in a wheelchair and to go out on his feet. Heads of homes combine the roles of staff manager, domestic organiser, nurse and social worker. All staff have a part to play in promoting the social and emotional well-being of their residents as well as providing the care services.

Many local authorities now provide in-service training for residential care staff, and also allow them to attend the day release courses approved by the Central Council for Education and Training in Social Work (CCETSW) that are run by local colleges. Such courses place great emphasis on knowing the resources of one's own department and local organisations. The invitation to give a lecture on such a course should be received with enthusiasm, for it gives the worker an opportunity to explain his or her own role, and to meet colleagues with whom he could well be working in the near future.

Day care staff

There is again no formal training requirement for the staff in day care establishments for the physically handicapped; however, specific types of day centres do seek appropriately trained staff. For example, day training centres for adult mentally handicapped are appropriately managed by holders of the certificate issued by the National Association of Teachers of the Mentally Handicapped or by Registered Nurses for the Mentally Subnormal (RNMS). Similarly, work centres for

Physical handicap and society

the physically handicapped are often managed by occupational therapists or by craftsmen with industrial experience. Day centres for the mentally ill may have Registered Mental Nurses on the staff. The CSS is now beginning to be seen as an appropriate form of training as well.

Managers of work centres are very much managers in the industrial sense, for they have to organise the work of both staff and clients, co-ordinate transport and obtain orders for work from local industry. Other staff act as instructors and supervisors, may help with feeding and toileting where required and take an interest in the social and emotional well-being of the persons attending the centre. Good day centres also offer counselling and group work. Day centre staff have the opportunity to get to know the clients really well, for they see them regularly over long periods of time. A social worker aiming to assess the needs of a handicapped person already attending a centre can be greatly helped by consulting the centre staff.

Day centre staff can also take part in comprehensive rehabilitation programmes and handicapped people (including mentally ill and mentally handicapped) can be enabled to move on to a sheltered workshop and even open employment after a spell in a good day centre.

The family aide

Some social services departments employ family aides, who can go into the home in times of stress – living in if necessary – to prevent the collapse of the family and to help keep children and disabled or elderly adults out of care. Aides usually give general support to the family for a short period only. They can help with the planning and execution of home management, child care and simple patient care while the family is learning to cope again after illness or social disaster. They can play a very important part in the rehabilitation of a disabled person and provide a bridge between hospital care and independence in the community. In the case of mentally ill parents and disadvantaged families, aides play an educative role too, teaching the parents the essentials of budgeting, child care and home management.

This is essentially a short-term service intended to tide the client or family over a crisis period. Aides do not take over the work and responsibilities but rather they step in to enable

82

the family to cope better. Where no resolution of the problem seems in sight, then the disabled person concerned may be more appropriately placed in residential care.

Aides have no formal training but are trained "on the job" by their departments. They are usually mature people with plenty of practical experiences of life, often having nursed their own elderly relatives.

The social work assistant

The role of the social work assistant varies considerably between social work departments. Sometimes different teams in the same local authority use them in different ways. Some authorities use them to assist social workers, taking over the less demanding aspects of their cases, and some give them caseloads of their own, though usually not of the most difficult cases. There is no formal training requirement for social work assistants, but most local authorities run in-service training programmes, and many technical colleges have day release schemes which they can attend.

In areas with a higher than average incidence of social deprivation (in other words slums, problem families and crime) child care and family casework occupies most of the social worker's time, and the assistants can become used as social workers for the elderly, blind, deaf and disabled. CCETSW has at last begun to recognise this, and is including provision for social work assistants in CSS courses.

Some departments' social work assistants are given the task of long-term support and supervision of clients once the initial assessment has been done and the urgent needs met by the social workers or the occupational therapists. Often acute problems such as need for rehousing, adaptations to the home, advice on family problems and arranging employment services can be dealt with fairly quickly and the case can then be closed. However, when an elderly or handicapped (or even socially inadequate) client needs keeping an eye on because of constant need for care, or because of a deteriorating condition, then it may be appropriate for the case to be handed over to the social work assistant.

Many social work assistants are recruited from the ranks of mature housewives, who wish to return to work but who cannot or do not wish to go to college and train. Often they have cared for elderly relatives of their own as well as bringing up a family and their experience of family situations gives them an ability to care and understand. Less mobile than the social workers they often develop a long-term relationship with the clients and gain a knowledge of local customs and local affairs which is a great asset to the department.

The National Health Service: the primary health care team

The primary health care team is so called because it represents the patient's first and perhaps only contact with the health service. Consisting of the family doctor and the community nursing services, the team caters for the health needs of the community. In large towns, teams often work from a health centre where, in addition to doctors, nurses and health visitors, there may be visiting chiropodists, opticians and eye specialists, hearing specialists, and the various doctors and nurses who run ante-natal and infant welfare clinics. Not all doctors are in partnerships using health centres, especially in rural areas. However, they still work closely with other members of the team.

In order to give continuity of care to the patient, district nurses and health visitors are attached to a general practitioner. The members of the primary care team meet regularly to decide what is best to be done for the patient, and which member of the team should take on the case. They may also decide that other services such as home help and meals on wheels are needed and then they would refer the case to the social services department.

The general practitioner

This is the patient's own family doctor, who specialises in general medicine. Except in an emergency, this is the first doctor that the patient should see, for he is trained to examine and diagnose and then decide what form of treatment is necessary. Often, the GP will treat minor ailments and minor injuries himself. He is also first on the scene in many cases of stroke, heart attack and serious illnesses occurring when the patient is at home. In the case of serious illness, he will arrange for the patient to be admitted to hospital. He will also pass on to an appropriate specialist cases which require more specialist knowledge, or specialised tests, before diagnosis can be made and will be informed of the outcome.

Healthy patients may also visit their GP to request routine

innoculations, family planning advice and the first report of an expected baby.

The community nurse

Community nurses, or district nurses as they are better known, may be State Registered Nurses with extra community nursing training, State Enrolled Nurses or nursing auxiliaries trained on the job. Cases are allocated to them according to complexity of skills needed, the auxiliaries often taking on tasks such as bathing the elderly at home, and simple bed nursing under the direction of a trained nurse. State Registered Nurses in the community have the status of a Sister, and each has responsibility for her own patients, though for administrative purposes she is responsible to the District Nursing Officer.

District nurses perform practical nursing tasks in the patient's own home, generally supervise the progress of the case, teach the family how to help, and see that a supply of dressings and other medical supplies is maintained. Almost all the nursing tasks done in a hospital can also be carried out in the home. Nurses may be asked to change dressings and take out stitches after patients with minor injuries or who have had minor operations have been discharged from hospital. They may visit daily to give injections to diabetics too old or too blind to inject themselves. They may visit the elderly to dress ulcers or to help with management of catheters. They may supervise and assist with the care of patients being nursed in bed at home by their families, in particular the terminally ill. Throughout their involvement with the case they are expected to observe and monitor the patient's progress, report if necessary to the doctor, and to inform the social services department if social problems are found. Nursing auxiliaries may be used for less skilled jobs such as bathing, hair washing and care of nails and feet.

District nurses accept patients only from the GP to whom they are attached and from hospitals. As they are treating patients, it is always necessary that a medical diagnosis be made before they go into the case.

The health visitor

Health visitors have qualified in nursing and midwifery before going on to take further training in community health. Their role is to educate and advise on health matters and much of their work is done with mothers of children under five and with old people. They do not undertake practical nursing tasks such as giving injections and dressing wounds, as this is done by the district nurses.

Health visitors are attached to general practitioners, but each is responsible for her own patients. She may accept referrals from any source: doctors, social workers, neighbours and patients themselves. Trained to assess medical as well as social problems, she will then often pass cases on to other people, such as home help organisers, chiropodists and so on.

The health visitor's role is essentially a preventative one. When a new baby is born, she visits the home soon after the mother leaves hospital, and shows herself to be willing to help and advise on babycare matters. Often the mother is coping very well, and does not need help, but when problems arise the right sort of advice can prevent minor worries – such as sleepless nights, nappy rash and difficulties in feeding – from escalating into major catastrophes. A combination of depressed mother and noisy unco-operative baby presents a great risk of baby battering, and the health visitor's training in spotting approaching depression and sorting out baby problems can do a lot to prevent this occurring. Mothers of disabled babies need extra help. Feeding, sleeping and bathing difficulties, added to the inevitable distress of seeing one's baby handicapped, can make a very tired and depressed mother. Even good and sensible mothers can be rather nervous of their ability to cope with a very new baby, and the health visitor's reassurance can do a lot to help the mother to stop worrying needlessly and to enjoy looking after her baby.

Health visitors often make routine visits to old people to make sure that they are able to keep themselves warm, fed and as well as possible, particularly in the winter. They can advise on diet as well as general health matters, and old people living alone, not able to go far to shop and not really up to complicated cookery, may need to be persuaded to accept meals on wheels. They may go to visit young adults, too, if they need advice and sometimes the doctor will ask them to keep an eye on physically handicapped persons and patients suffering from depression.

The health visitor's role has been compared to that of a minesweeper, cruising routinely around in the hope of detecting any problem that might be floating about, so that she can defuse it before it goes off and damages somebody.

The National Health Service: hospital staff

Referrals to any of the hospital and clinic staff described should always be made through the patient's own doctor. This ensures that a medical opinion is available and that all relevant medical information is passed on. It is, however, very useful for social workers and residential staff to be in contact with members of other professions working with one of their clients. Quite often a preliminary telephone conversation will serve both to introduce the staff to each other and to find out the sort of information one's colleague would like to be sent.

The dietician

Dieticians are trained to apply the science of nutrition to health care both in hospitals and in the community. State Registration is required before they can practise, and qualification is by degree or diploma course lasting four years. Students may take an eighteen-month course if already qualified in nursing, institutional management or home economics. Dieticians have studied the theoretical aspects of nutrition and food presentation, and also the skills of teaching and persuasion (it is no good giving the patient a special diet if you can not persuade him to keep to it!).

Patients suffering from diabetes, kidney complaints and obesity need to be taught how to cope with diets which seem strange at first. They also need to understand why it is so important that they follow them. A good dietician can show them how to present their food in attractive ways so that dieting is less of a hardship, and therefore more likely to be done. The dietician has studied psychology and is aware of its importance at all times.

Dieticians are also concerned with the "normal" diet and can advise hospitals, women's groups, school meals services and so on. Some are attached to community health clinics and lecture to slimmers, expectant mothers, immigrants unfamiliar with British food and welfare staff of all kinds.

The chiropodist

For many elderly patients, the regular attention of a chiropodist can make the difference between being able to walk and immobility. Old people's feet often become malformed and calloused, and toe-nails can become too hard to cut, even for those who can still reach. In-growing toe-nails, corns and bunions contribute to the misery of aching feet and, added to the stiff joints and poor balance that comes with old age, really cripple the patient.

The chiropodist, with his special knowledge of the anatomy of feet and legs, treatment and care of the feet and the making and fitting of appliances, can literally "keep the patient on his feet". The NHS recognises this and employs chiropodists in hospitals, clinics, health centres and special schools. Some attend elderly and handicapped people in their own homes. Unfortunately, there seems to be a never-ending shortage of qualified chiropodists and in some areas priority has to be given to old people, handicapped children and expectant mothers. There are many chiropodists in private practice, but clients attending should be advised to make sure that the practitioner concerned is a qualified chiropodist.

Much of the work consists of cutting nails, trimming corns, strapping bunions and applying pads to correct foot deformities. With children it may be necessary to strap crooked toes to encourage them to grow straight and to apply pads, braces and special shoes to deformed feet which prevent the child from walking properly.

It is particularly important for social services staff to see that diabetic patients get good foot treatment, especially those whose sight is none too good. Advanced diabetics are very prone to foot problems and may suffer from ulcers, poor circulation, toe-nail deformities and eventually – if not looked after properly – gangrene. A social worker attending any diabetic should *always* enquire if there are any foot problems, and see that the client is sent to a chiropodist if necessary.

State Registered Chiropodists have to have completed a three-year course of study and intending students must have two "A" Levels.

The speech therapist

Speech therapists assess, diagnose and treat disorders of speech and language. They are trained to understand the anatomy and physiology of speech and hearing, to devise exercises and treatments aimed at overcoming defects and to relate their work to the psychology of language concepts.

They can be found working in hospitals, clinics, health centres, medical rehabilitation centres and special schools. Many work with children, helping them overcome speech defects caused by congenital abnormalities, mental handicap and social deprivation. Other speech therapists work with adults, especially stroke patients who can lose both the power of speech and the mental ability to put words together in a meaningful pattern. Patients who have had part of the larynx removed have to be taught to speak again in a totally different way.

The importance of speech therapy cannot be overestimated. Children with speech and language disorders have great problems in learning and in getting their wants understood. They have difficulty in making friends and the resultant isolation can result in emotional disturbances later. The adult who cannot speak properly is grossly disadvantaged in any social situation, and his closest relationships can become strained. Good speech therapy applied at the right time can prevent these disorders arising.

Speech therapists qualify on degree or diploma courses lasting three years or more. Entry requirements vary, but all courses demand at least five "O" Levels and two "A" Levels. Unfortunately, there seems again to be a permanent shortage of these useful people.

The occupational therapist

The role of the occupational therapist has already been described in the section above on social services staff. However, the occupational therapist's role in hospital is different, and in addition to providing aids to rehabilitation they undertake much more remedial therapy with the patient. Their main duty is to help sick and injured patients to recover lost skills, or to develop alternative means of performing tasks when this is not possible. People recovering from road traffic accidents, strokes and long illnesses may need to be taught again how to dress, wash, cook and clean the house. Throughout her period of contact with the patient, the therapist is assessing his ability to cope with everyday tasks prior to returning home.

Hospital occupational therapists also teach and organise crafts and workshop activities specially planned for each patient in order to strengthen and restore control to injured upper und lower limbs. They work very closely with physiotherapists in this, aiming to restore the patient to full activity.

Occupational therapists also work in psychiatric hospitals and clinics where they play an important part in the treatment team. They provide a variety of practical situations and activities within which patients are enabled to discover and explore their strengths and weaknesses and to rebuild patterns of work and daily living. Group activities and social training programmes help patients to examine and develop their ability to relate successfully to others. Hobbies, games, creative activities such as art and crafts and sport help patients to develop interests and to structure their leisure time.

The physiotherapist

Physiotherapists are trained to treat illnesses or injuries by physical means. Their three years of training in anatomy, physiology and treatment methods enable them to work in hospitals, clinics and schools for the disabled, where they help the patient to attain or regain lost bodily functions.

Patients who are recovering from fractures, dislocations and torn muscles can be helped to regain full function by the application of heat and cold, electrical and ultrasonic treatments, manipulation and by the practice of carefully designed exercises. Handicapped children can be taught to sit, stand and walk correctly, and when this is not possible exercises, appliances and correct positioning can prevent their deformities from becoming worse. Permanently disabled adults, such as those suffering from stroke, rheumatic diseases and various types of paralysis, can be helped to remain active longer and painful and disfiguring secondary deformities which arise when limbs are not used can be prevented. Physiotherapists also advise patients on the simple treatments and exercises they should do at home between clinic visits and they advise parents how to help treat and exercise disabled children at home.

Less well known to the general public are techniques such as postural drainage, which is used to help chest patients expel mucus from the lungs, and the use of electrical stimulation to help post-operative patients – particularly gynaecology and prostatectomy patients – recover bladder control.

Elderly patients with increasing infirmity should not be written off as incurable until physiotherapy has been tried.

Social services staff in contact with infirm elderly patients can always consult the patient's own doctor if they think therapy might help.

The layman tends to associate physiotherapy with massage but massage on its own is not used much nowadays as it is of limited value, modern techniques being much more effective.

The remedial gymnast

The training of remedial gymnasts is in some ways similar to that of physiotherapists, for both use physical means to develop and restore function to damaged tissues. However, the remedial gymnast relies much more on exercises and games to achieve improvement and does not give electrical or manipulative treatments.

Remedial gymnasts are found working in hospitals and medical rehabilitation centres, especially where young spinal injury patients are treated. They are usually found working in conjunction with doctors, physiotherapists, social workers and employment officers, who are all trying to get the patient back to work. Some remedial gymnasts are employed in schools for disabled children where they organise games which are fun to play as well as beneficial. Some work in subnormality hospitals and help to keep the patients occupied as well as fit.

In order to qualify as a remedial gymnast, students must complete a three-year course, which includes anatomy, physiology and physical education. Normally five "O" Levels are required for entry, and intending students need to be very fit and good at games.

10 The duties of social services departments

The acts of Parliament described in Chapter 8 lay down the services to handicapped people that should be offered by the local authority social services department. This chapter describes in more detail the way that most social services departments carry out their obligations for the care and rehabilitation of chronically sick and disabled people.

Assessment and advice

When the department receives notification of a disabled person who needs a service, it is the responsibility of the area social work team to send someone to visit the person in his own home and assess the need for services. The worker can then look at the disabled person's living situation, discuss aids and services with him and help him to decide which of the services available will best meet his needs. At the same time, the worker takes the opportunity to make sure that the disabled person is aware of the other services and concessions available to him from other sources, such as social security or one of the local voluntary bodies.

Either a social worker or an occupational therapist can make this initial assessment of the case. If the problem seems to be that of severe disability requiring complicated gadgetry or major reorganisation of the home, then the occupational therapist is most usually sent. If the problem seems to be more to do with the emotional consequences of disability and their effects upon the family, then it is more appropriate for a social worker to visit the client. In practice there is considerable overlap between the roles of these two professions. Both may advise on welfare benefits, arrange for holidays and call in other services; the social worker often advises on the simpler aids and the occupational therapist is well aware of the normal emotional reactions to disability. In complicated cases it is not uncommon to find both the social worker and the occupational therapist involved and working together to give the best possible service to the disabled person.

Registration

The Chronically Sick and Disabled Persons Act 1970 requires the local authority to maintain a register of disabled people living within its boundaries. It is usual for the worker making first contact with the case to explain the registration procedures to the disabled person. Handicapped people are not obliged to register and they are still entitled to most local authority services if they do not. However, some concessions, such as the parking disc and rent and rate rebates, require proof of disability and the applicant who is not registered will have to produce a letter from his doctor before being allowed to receive the benefit.

A medical certificate is not required for registration if the disability is recognisable on lay inspection (possession of a wheelchair for example, or obvious walking difficulties). The social worker or occupational therapist can fill in the form and have the client registered immediately. (For registration as a blind or partially sighted person a different procedure is required and the patient must be examined by an eye specialist first.) Registration as disabled with a local authority is not the same as registration with the Department of Employment. For employment purposes, the person about to be registered must be capable of some kind of work and must be either working or looking for work. The social services register is aimed at identifying people likely to need help from the social services department, and many of the people registered will be unable to work or be over retiring age, or be housewives.

There are three categories of handicapped registration: very severely handicapped, severely handicapped and appreciably handicapped. Classification depends upon the degree of loss of independent function; for example, someone unable to walk, to get out of bed unaided and to wash and dress himself would be registered as very severely handicapped, someone able to do more for himself but not independent would come into the severely handicapped category, and a patient able to do most things, but with difficulty, would be considered appreciably handicapped.

Loss of part of a limb or an eye does not necessarily imply loss of independence and therefore, persons with only one good eye, or who have lost some of the fingers on one hand are not necessarily eligible for registration. It should be remembered, too, that persons suffering from severe heart complaints or bronchitis may be very much incapacitated by these and are therefore eligible for registration as disabled by the local authority.

Help in the home

The aim of social services intervention is to help the disabled person to keep his independence as long as possible, and to this end both aids to self-care and help with household tasks can be provided.

The department can provide better access to the home for wheelchairs, and handrails, toilet aids and bath aids for people capable of moving about. Aids to self-care such as special shoe laces, long-handled combs and shoe horns, stocking pullers and so forth can be issued on request. For those able to run their homes aids such as tap turners, screwtop-jar openers and special cutlery and crockery can be provided and advice given on their use. More detailed information on aids and their selection is given in Chapters 14 and 15.

Home help services

For those who are less able, home help may be necessary to keep the disabled person in the community. When a handicapped person cannot cope with all or some of the tasks required to run a home the area team can send the home help organiser to visit and assess for domestic help. The organiser needs to see all over the house and to make an estimate of how much the patient can be expected to do to help himself before deciding how much home help time to allow. The service is usually free to persons who are dependent upon the old age pension or upon national insurance benefits for their sole income. People who have a private income may be assessed and pay for the home help according to their means. Payment is made direct to the department and not to the home help herself, for she is paid a guaranteed hourly rate irrespective of the means of the client.

Home helps themselves usually have more than one client to see, depending upon the number of hours they work. Whenever possible the same help visits the same client so that they both have a chance to get to know each other. Often they become quite attached to each other, a situation which helps the handicapped person become less despondent about having to be helped.

The home help is expected to perform all the usual household duties such as cleaning, laundry and shopping. Sometimes she cooks the lunch, and leaves suitable cold dishes ready for the days when she is not expected to call. In recent years the home help has come to be regarded as much more than a domestic worker. She may be the only person the disabled person ever sees and as such provides valuable links with other services and with the local community. The home help is ultimately responsible to the home help organiser, and is expected to report any problems to her. In this way, things that go wrong are reported to the area team for social work intervention. Because of this, most departments now train their own home helps. Those departments that run training courses for their home helps find that many requests for aids and services come from the helps themselves as they use their knowledge to give the utmost assistance to their clients.

There is a strong feeling throughout the country now that the home-help service should be extended to provide other services and to cover unsocial hours. Many local authorities are providing services such as the night-sitter service, neighbourly helps (who call in to perform specific tasks such as getting a person up) and assistants who can actually live in to help the family cope for a few days. Some authorities have a comprehensive home care service aimed at keeping the old or disabled person in the community, and whose staff can provide the sort of care normally expected from a relative. Such help can be provided as short-term care to help a patient recovering after a spell in hospital, or as a long-term project. Many such schemes are experimental and enquiries for help should be made locally.

Meals on wheels

Many elderly and handicapped people receive meals on wheels either daily, or on regular days every week. All social services departments are supposed to provide this service, though they have discretion on deciding needs and priorities for individual cases.

The person requiring the service can make the request via the social worker or the home help to the meals on wheels organiser, usually a centrally based administrative officer, and hot lunches will be delivered to the door as soon as there is a place on the round available. Some areas have a waiting list for the service. A small charge is made, which is well below the cost of producing the meal. No assessments are made and everybody pays the same. The client pays when the meal is delivered, or once a week to the meals on wheels staff. Meals on wheels services were originally staffed by voluntary organisations such as the WRVS. Nowadays, however, most local authorities pay their own staff of drivers and assistants, though many of these are the same people who used to run the service as volunteers.

The incontinence laundry service

Several acts of Parliament permit local authorities and the area health boards of the NHS to provide a laundry service for the bed linen of incontinent patients. The service can be provided by either agency, or both working together. However, it is not compulsory, and so local provision varies. Where it exists it is free of charge.

The patient or his family is expected only to rinse out the soiled linen before sending it to the laundry, and it will be returned ready for use. This service is of tremendous benefit to the families of incontinent patients, who otherwise would have to spend a lot of time in laundering linen, and in the case of the elderly, might not be able to cope with the heavy work involved.

Telephones

The Chronically Sick and Disabled Persons Act 1970 makes it the duty of social services departments to provide for the installation and rental of telephones for the severely sick and disabled who cannot afford their own. This service was originally intended both as a means of summoning help in an emergency and as a way of avoiding isolation, but financial stringencies have made some authorities give priority to the need to summon help. As the criteria for provision are left to the discretion of the local authority concerned, standards of service vary and in some places only the very disabled who live alone, and who cannot go out, are helped to have a telephone installed.

Any social worker arranging for an elderly person to have a telephone installed should be sure that the client knows how to work it, for the elderly are often a little nervous about using gadgetry. Some indication of the cost of calls should be given, too, for clients are expected to pay for the cost of their own calls. It is reported that some people whose rental is paid by the local authority make no calls at all, either because they don't know how to use the 'phone, or because they are afraid of running up a big bill. The whole procedure would be pointless if the client could not use the telephone in an emergency because he had never tried to use it before. (Conversely, a few people need to be reminded that the social services department will not pay for private calls and that running up huge debts will result in their 'phone being cut off!)

Occupation in the home

The disabled person who finds it difficult to go out might well like to be visited by the domiciliary craft instructor. The acts of Parliament concerned make it the duty of social services departments to provide occupation "in their own homes or elsewhere", for disabled people who have difficulty in occupying their time. The service is intended to provide diversion rather than paid work, though the proficient can make some money by the sale of finished work.

The craft instructor has a regular round of visits in which she demonstrates work methods, supplies materials and arranges for the sale of articles made. Some clients require simply to be kept supplied with wool for knitting, while others more adventurous, or perhaps blessed with better hand control, make trays, baskets, jewellery, mosaics, lampshades, dolls, soft toys and rugs.

Craft instructors are valuable colleagues of the social worker for they see the clients regularly and can report any changes in the situation. A person visiting the home soon becomes the recipient of confidences and many difficult problems come to light in the relaxed and friendly atmosphere of the craft teacher's visit. The craft itself is valuable not only as an occupation but because it provides an opportunity to make something which is of real use to someone else.

97

Handicraft classes and day centres

Regular classes and special day centres are other ways of providing occupation and are especially valuable to those who otherwise do not go outside their homes. They help to provide a more normal pattern to the day and are especially valuable to the young physically handicapped person who is too disabled to hold down a job. The way these services are provided varies greatly according to local need, local policy and local tradition. They range from weekly clubs and classes run in a hired church hall to full-scale, full-time occupation centres. The type of activity ranges from hobbies, games and entertainments to craft and even contracted industrial work. Educational activities, too, can be provided in some areas. Some centres cater for people under retirement age only and others accept clients from any age group.

Where craft or industrial work is done, there is opportunity to earn some money though, as the aim of the centres is occupation rather than employment, earnings are not high. The level of earnings is always kept below that at which social security benefits would be jeopardised. Because of this some clients feel that they are working for nothing and that "the council" is making a vast profit at their expense. Sometimes it is necessary to explain to one's client that people who are taken by ambulance to work at 10.30 a.m., who leave again at 3.00 a.m. and who do as much gossiping as they like in between, are not really earning a wage. The actual costs of running these centres greatly outweigh the minor profits sometimes made when two or three good workers get cracking on a good industrial contract.

Work centres should not be confused with sheltered workshops, even though some of them may be called workshops. The main difference is that in a sheltered workshop, disabled people are treated as workers, not clients. They clock in, do a normal day's work under factory conditions, and take home a proper wage at the end of the week. In the work centre, the pace is much more leisurely and is geared to the need for occupation in those too old or too disabled to work, even under sheltered conditions.

Social clubs

Some local authorities organise clubs where handicapped people can meet their friends (and others), play games such as bingo or dominoes, be entertained by singers and musicians, and enjoy a good tea and a gossip. More often, clubs of this type are run by voluntary bodies, though the local authority may offer the loan of a hall, help with the running costs and provide transport for those unable to get there on their own. There are some very enterprising clubs around, often run by disabled people themselves. Sports, games, lectures, debates and film shows provide occupation and stimulation for the members. Sometimes the local authority lends speakers from the adult education, museum and library services. More information on sport and recreation is given in Chapter 24, it being simply the purpose of this chapter to remind the reader that local authorities have a duty to provide recreation for disabled people under the terms of the Chronically Sick and Disabled Persons Act of 1970.

Holidays for the disabled

Local authorities are empowered to provide assistance with the cost of holidays and to organise holiday schemes of their own for elderly and disabled people. These may be taken either because the client needs a holiday or because his relatives need a break from looking after him. More information is given in Chapter 23.

Residential care

All local authorities must provide homes for elderly and handicapped persons incapable of looking after themselves, or who have no home of their own and no likelihood of getting one. They are also bound to provide hostel accommodation for the handicapped where necessary. These duties date from the National Assistance Act 1948, though thirty years does not seem to have done away with the waiting lists for places.

All local authorities run old people's homes for the elderly who are no longer capable of caring for themselves, but who do not need the full-scale nursing given by a hospital. As most of the disabled are of pensionable age, most of those needing care are able to be catered for in local authority homes.

However, these homes are not suitable for the younger disabled who require more interest and stimulation than that provided by the slow-moving atmosphere of the old people's establishments. As the demand for places by young disabled is small, most local authorities discharge their duties by arranging to place their younger clients needing care in one of the homes run by private and voluntary bodies, and they also pay the fees. There is almost always a waiting list for places in good residential homes, and also for hostels. More information on residential care, including short-stay and holiday accommodation, is given in Chapters 23 and 25.

11 The work of the major voluntary organisations

The professional person working with the disabled will quickly realise the importance of the voluntary organisations, and no social worker will be able to give a good service to her clients without knowing the resources of the national and local charities. Local voluntary groups usually keep their own local social services department informed of their activities. We are giving here a list (not exhaustive) of the major national charities for the disabled, together with a brief description of the work they do. Their addresses are given and their staff are always ready to send further information about their activities. Further references to the work of the charities in providing rehabilitation centres, holidays, recreation and leisure and residential homes are given in Part Four of this book.

Age Concern
  Bernard Sunley House, 60 Pitcairn Road, Mitcham, Surrey CR4 3LL

Aimed at "promoting the welfare of the aged", this charity organises local schemes for voluntary visiting, luncheon clubs and day centres and also researches the needs of the elderly and campaigns for better services.

Association for Spina Bifida and Hydrocephalus
  Tavistock House North, Tavistock Square, London WC1H 9HJ

This organisation aims to advise and support people suffering from these conditions, and the parents of affected children. Parents are kept in touch by the magazine *Link* and also by local groups. ASBAH also gives advice and publishes booklets on holidays, clothing, play materials, equipment, education and employment.

The Association to Combat Huntington's Chorea (COMBAT)
"Lyndhurst", Lower Hampton Road, Sunbury-on-Thames, Middlesex TW16 5PR

Exists to help families in which Huntington's Chorea occurs, by offering advice on the medical, practical and psychological aspects of the disease. The association fosters research into the condition and campaigns for improved facilities and benefits for sufferers. It runs a holiday home in Theydon Bois, Essex, and can give individual counselling in the London area.

Association of Disabled Professionals
The Stables, 73 Pound Road, Banstead, Surrey, SM7 2HU

This is an interest and pressure group which seeks to promote rehabilitation, employment and social integration of disabled people, by giving advice to disabled students and members of the professions.

Back Pain Association
Grundy House, Somerset Road, Teddington, Middlesex TW11 8TD

The Back Pain Association was set up in 1968 to sponsor research into the causes, treatment and prevention of injuries to the back, a major source of pain and absenteeism from work. As well as financing research, the association organises seminars for doctors and other professionals, produces leaflets and posters showing ways to avoid back injury and provides advice to patients with back trouble.

British Association of the Hard of Hearing
44 Grays Inn Road, London WC1X 8LR

This group exists to give advice and help to those with hearing problems, both by magazine and via local groups. It also organises sports and outdoor pursuits.

British Deaf Association
38 Victoria Place, Carlisle CA1 1HU

The association has branches throughout the country which run clubs and sporting activities. It also publishes a journal, advises parents of deaf children, and maintains homes for the elderly deaf.

British Diabetic Association
10 Queen Anne Street, London W1M 0BD

This group promotes research into diabetes and provides information to professional staff. It also informs and educates diabetic patients via its magazine *Balance* (also produced on tape for the blind) and a variety of very useful books and leaflets. A lot of work is done to help diabetic children learn to cope with the complaint, and the BDA publishes games and children's booklets and also organises summer holiday camps where children can enjoy themselves while learning how to manage their diets, injections and urine tests for themselves.

British Epilepsy Association
Crowthorne House, New Wokingham Road, Wokingham, Berkshire RG11 3AY

This association was founded in 1950, to promote research into the condition, to act as a pressure group for epileptics and to advise and support patients and their families. It organises study courses, supplies speakers and publishes leaflets and films. Individual patients can write to the Information Unit for advice.

British Polio Fellowship
Bell Close, West End Road, Ruislip, Middlesex HA4 6LP

Promotes the welfare of people disabled by poliomyelitis, by advising and helping in local groups and via a quarterly journal. It also runs sheltered workshops and a variety of holiday schemes.

British Red Cross Society
9 Grosvenor Crescent, London SW1X 7GJ

This is part of an international welfare association, which provides medical care and relief for victims of war, famine and disaster. In Britain its main functions are welfare services, nursing and first-aid, loan of equipment for the sick and disabled and provision of voluntary nursing auxiliaries and escorts for handicapped people cared for at home.

British Rheumatism and Arthritis Association
6, Grosvenor Crescent, London SW1X 7ER

This organisation provides information and advice to rheumatism sufferers, and also runs residential homes, flats and various holiday schemes (including self-catering accommodation).

The British Sports Association for the Disabled
Stoke Mandeville Sports Stadium for the Paralysed and Other Disabled, Harvey Road, Aylesbury, Buckinghamshire

This is the organising and co-ordinating body of sport for handicapped people, and has branches throughout the country. It organises a wide variety of sports, including competitive sports, and can also supply information on activities (such as angling) that do not require organised facilities. It is the British organising authority for the Disabled Olympics.

Brittle Bone Society
Mrs Margarget Grant, Secretary, 63 Byron Crescent, Dundee DD3 6SS

Consists of patients, parents and others concerned with the condition. It raises funds for research into inheritance and treatment and issues information and advice to members via the newsletter and by personal contact. The society employs an occupational therapist who can visit children in their own homes and advise on aids, adaptations and toys.

Chest, Heart and Stroke Association
Tavistock House North, Tavistock Square, London, WC1H 9JE

This association promotes research into heart, lung and circulatory diseases, and disseminates information to professional people and to patients and their families. It takes an active part in the rehabilitation of stroke patients by sponsoring and funding stroke clubs. It also publishes useful booklets for the layman on angina, coronary complaints, bronchitis, asthma, heart disease, high blood pressure and strokes.

Coeliac Society of Great British and Northern Ireland
  PO Box 181, London NW2 2QY

The Coeliac Society exists to advise patients, including children, who have been medically diagnosed as being sensitive to gluten (wheat protein), and may therefore have to spend much of their lives on a special diet. It publishes useful literature and recipe books, and can advise individual patients.

The Colostomy Welfare Group
  38/39 Eccleston Square, London SW1V 1PB

This group helps and advises on the management of colostomy by personal contacts and by producing literature.

Cystic Fibrosis Research Trust
  5 Blyth Road, Bromley, Kent BR1 3RS

Finances research, disseminates information, and runs local branches through which parents of children with the disease can be helped.

The Disability Alliance
  1 Cambridge Terrace, London NW1 4VL

The Disability Alliance is a federation of more than fifty organisations, united in the view that there should be an allowance paid as of right to all disabled people. The alliance continues to campaign for one type of disability allowance irrespective of age, sex or origin of handicap, which will bring the income of the disabled up to the level of the able-bodied. It conducts research and publishes booklets to support its claim, and also brings out the invaluable *Disability Rights Handbook* to help the handicapped get the best out of the existing provisions.

The Disabled Drivers' Association
  Ashwellthorpe Hall, Ashwellthorpe, Norwich, Norfolk NR16 1EX

Exists to help and advise handicapped motorists, to make their views known and it also runs sporting events, a holiday hotel for members and operates car-ferry concessions.

Disabled Drivers' Motor Club Ltd
9 Park Parade, Gunnersbury Avenue, London W3 9BD

Supplies magazine information, advice and ferry concessions to members.

Disablement Income Group
Attlee House, Toynbee Hall, 28 Commercial Street, London E1 6LR

Known as DIG, this organisation campaigns for adequate social security benefits for all handicapped people and also publishes an excellent guide to services and information. There are many local groups.

Disabled Living Foundation
346 Kensington High Street, London W14 8NS

The DLF is a charitable trust set up to provide information and advice on all aspects of daily life for handicapped people. It organises a comprehensive standing exhibition of aids (one in London and one in Newcastle), publishes numerous information leaflets on clothing, recreation, domestic design, incontinence and access and sends indexed information lists on aids services and publications to the organisations who pay a subscription. Any disabled person can obtain advice free at any time and may visit the exhibition to try out aids and equipment.

The Family Fund
c/o Joseph Rowntree Memorial Trust, Beverley House, Shipton Road, York, YO3 6RB

The fund was set up on government recommendation, to help the families of severely handicapped children under 16. Help can only be given in instances where social security or local authority services are inappropriate. See p. 219 for more details.

The Friedreich's Ataxia Group
155 Great Portland Street, London W1

This organisation raises funds for research into the disease. It also helps the families of children with the disease by encouraging local groups and supplying information via booklets and newsletter.

Greater London Association for the Disabled (GLAD)
  1 Thorpe Close, London W10 5XL

This association co-ordinates the activities of groups for the handicapped throughout London and also publishes the quarterly *Glad News* and disseminates useful information. It acts as a pressure group in London, holding regular seminars on various aspects of disability in society.

Haemophilia Society
  16 Trinity Street, PO Box 9, London SE1 1DE

Information and advice, local groups and financial help for haemophiliacs and their families.

Handcrafts Advisory Association for the Disabled
  183 Queensway, London W2

This is a voluntary body which provides short courses for instructors and also organises craft competitions for disabled people.

Help the Aged
  32 Dover Street, London W1A 2AP

Help the Aged is an international organisation, active in all fields of old people's welfare. Overseas it organises housing, feeding and medical care, especially in disaster areas. In Britain, it runs sheltered housing schemes and day centres, and publishes the monthly newspaper *Yours* which gives information and advice to the elderly.

Ileostomy Association of Great Britain and Northern Ireland
  Amblehurst House, Chobham, Woking, Surrey

Provides information, advice and support to people about to undergo, or who have already had, an ileostomy operation.

Invalid Children's Aid Association
  126 Buckingham Palace Road, London SW1W 9SB

ICAA runs a worldwide research information and advisory service to parents of handicapped children. In Britain, it runs schools for asthmatics and for speech- and language-disordered children, playgroups for handicapped toddlers and, in the London area only, has visiting social workers.

Jewish Association for the Physically Handicapped
  14 Soho Street, London W1V 6HB

Provides social clubs and holidays for handicapped people of the Jewish faith.

Joint Committee on Mobility for the Disabled
  Peter Large, MBE, Chairman, 14 Birch Way, Warlingham, Surrey, CR3 9DA

This is a consortium of organisations concerned with disability. It collects and distributes information on matters such as access and travel. It also represents the disabled viewpoint and advises government departments on all matters of mobility for the physically handicapped.

The Mastectomy Association
  1 Colworth Road, Croydon, Surrey CR0 7AD

Gives advice and support of a non-medical nature to women who have had a breast removed, or who are awaiting the operation. It also publishes useful booklets and leaflets for patients and their families.

Multiple Sclerosis Society of Great Britain and Northern Ireland
  4 Tachbrook Street, London SW1V 1SJ

This organisation finances research into the disease and gives practical help to sufferers. Local groups run social and fund-raising events and the national organisation publishes a journal and information sheets, and also runs holiday homes, including some for patients who need nursing care. "Crack" is the young arm of the MS Society and it promotes the welfare and social needs of young patients, who still belong to the main society.

Muscular Dystrophy Group of Great Britain
  Nattrass House, 35 Macaulay Road, London SW4 0QP

This group concentrates most of its efforts on research into the disease, but it also provides advice and literature for patients as well. It has a sub-section dealing with myasthenia gravis. There are over 300 local groups, providing social contact, advice and support for patients and families. The *Muscular Dystrophy Handbook* gives useful information on the disease and provides a lot of advice on housing, holidays, education, employment and leisure activities.

National Association for Deaf/Blind and Rubella Handicapped
164 Cromwell Lane, Coventry, West Midlands CV4 8AP

This association has a national newsletter and local support groups for parents of rubella (German measles) children, who are often physically handicapped as well as deaf and/or blind. It also publishes useful leaflets and can lend films and speakers to interested organisations.

National Association for the Welfare of Children in Hospital
Exton House, 7 Exton Street, London SE1 8VE

NAWCH campaigns for better social treatment of child patients and publishes useful leaflets for parents and explanatory picture books for children about to go into hospital.

National Federation of St Raphael Clubs
11 Thurlin Road, Gaywood, Kings Lynn, Norfolk PE30 4QQ

This national body co-ordinates the activities of local social clubs for the disabled and publishes newsletters and advice leaflets. It also arranges holiday schemes for members.

The National Federation of Claimants' Unions
(East London Claimants' Union, Dame Colet House, Ben Jonson Road, London E1 keeps a list of local groups.)

Aims "to communicate and co-ordinate activities between bona fide claimants' unions." Local Claimants' Unions are made up of people who are receiving or have received supplementary benefits, or whose incomes are at or below SB level. The unions advise members on welfare rights, assist members to make claims and appeals and participate in a national campaign for "adequate income without means test for all people."

National Listening Library (Talking Books for the Handicapped)
49 Great Cumberland Place, London W1H 7LH

The library provides talking books and machines to people unable to read because of physical handicap. A charge is made for services, but most local authorities are willing to pay for this. (This scheme is not the same as that run for blind people by the RNIB.)

Northern Ireland Committee for the Handicapped
Northern Ireland Council of Social Service, 2 Annadale Avenue, Belfast BT7 3JH

Co-ordinates the work of agencies for the handicapped in Northern Ireland, and acts as a source of information.

Parkinson's Disease Society of the UK Ltd
81 Queens Road, London SW19 8NR

The society raises funds to sponsor medical research and also provides information and advice to patients and their families.

The Patients' Association
11 Dartmouth Street, London SW1H 9BN

Was founded in 1963 to campaign for the rights of patients as consumers. It publishes useful leaflets for people about to go into hospital or who are otherwise concerned about their rights or treatment as patients of the health service professions, and can advise individual patients. It also conducts campaigns on drug safety, hospital visiting, waiting times, privacy and use of patients in teaching.

PHAB (Physically Handicapped and Able-Bodied)
42 Devonshire Street, London W1N 1LN

PHAB is an organisation of youth clubs in which the physically handicapped and able-bodied join in on equal terms. Local PHAB clubs do all the things youth clubs do. National headquarters also run holiday instruction courses in sports, crafts, arts and other hobbies. There is a separate branch for people over 25.

Possum Users' Association
c/o Mr K. Winter, 14 Green Vale Drive, Tinsbury, Bath, Avon

PUA exists to keep Possum users in touch with one another, to give information and advice and to raise funds to help members buy equipment. PUA publishes *Possability*, a monthly newsletter, and information leaflets and posters. The Possum environmental control system is explained in Chapter 14.

*Rehabilitation Engineering Movement Advisory Panels
(REMAP)*
  c/o E. J. Lane, CEng, MIMechE, 2 Garrard Road, Banstead, Surrey

REMAP, an offshoot of RADAR, consists of panels of engineers, doctors and others who give their services voluntarily, in researching, advising and assisting on individual problems of disabled mobility. The projects undertaken so far have ranged from designing a device for opening a car door to producing complicated equipment for nursing a severely disabled hospital patient. The services are free, but the cost of materials and expenses should be met by the local social services department.

Royal Association for Disability and Rehabilitation (RADAR)
  25 Mortimer Street, London W1N 8AB

In 1977 the British Council for the Rehabilitation of the Disabled and the Central Council for the Disabled came together to form RADAR, as it is now known. RADAR incorporates a large number of local associations and is very active in all matters of concern to disabled people. It runs rehabilitation programmes for long-stay patients and has information and a long list of publications on housing, access, aids, mobility, travel and holidays. RADAR publishes a monthly bulletin of up-to-date information, available on annual subscription.

Royal National Institute for the Blind (RNIB)
  224 Great Portland Street, London W1N 6AA

The largest and most comprehensive body dealing with blindness in the United Kingdom; it deals with all matters relating to the care, welfare and rehabilitation of the visually handicapped. The RNIB runs schools, colleges, assessment and rehabilitation centres and holiday homes; it also markets aids and literature and runs an advisory and placement service on employment. The monthly journal *New Beacon* is the recognised journal of blind welfare in Britain.

Royal National Institute for the Deaf (RNID)
  105 Gower Street, London WC1E 6AH

The RNID offers information and advice to the deaf and hard of hearing. It publishes the monthly journal *Hearing* and leaflets on communication, hearing aids and other equipment. It also runs a training establishment and special school, and in general acts as a pressure group for better services.

St John Ambulance Brigade
1 Grosvenor Crescent, London SW1X 7EF

Mainly a first-aid and nursing organisation. Local groups of volunteers are trained to an approved standard and then run first-aid posts at public events and assist with nursing patients in their own homes. The Brigade also runs first-aid courses for the general public and provides escorts and nursing assistance for disabled people's outings, parties and holidays. St John cadets learn about hygiene and child care as well, and also enjoy recreational activities and games.

Scottish Council on Disability
18–19 Claremont Crescent, Edinburgh EH7 4QD

This body gives information and co-ordinates the work of organisations for the disabled in Scotland.

Shaftesbury Society
Shaftesbury House, 112 Regency Street, London SW1P 4AX

Maintains schools, residential homes and holiday centres and clubs for the disabled.

Spastics Society
12 Park Crescent, London W1N 4EQ

This is a very large charity, offering a comprehensive service to people suffering from cerebral palsy. It runs schools, colleges, assessment centres and residential homes and trains its own residential care staff to run them. It also runs holiday schemes of various sorts, and publishes lists of holidays run by several organisations. The Society publishes the monthly *Spastics News* and a long list of leaflets and booklets on aids, equipment, employment and social life, including an excellent one on courtship and marriage for the severely disabled.

SPOD (Committee on Sexual and Personal Relationships of the Disabled)
Brook House, 2–16 Torrington Place, London WC1E 7HN.

SPOD exists to promote awareness of the problems of sexual expression for the severely handicapped, and to offer advice to disabled people and the professions working with them on how these can be overcome. SPOD also sells useful literature and trains counsellors.

Spinal Injuries Association
  5 Crowndale Road, London NW1 1TU

This group provides advice to people who are paralysed from a spinal injury, and has literature on welfare rights and on self-care.

Toy Libraries Association
  Seabrook House, Wyllyotts Manor, Darkes Lane, Potters Bar, Hertfordshire, EN6 2HL

Co-ordinates and promotes toy libraries and trains volunteers to run them. The organisation can advise on toys suitable for both handicapped and able-bodied children.

Voluntary Council for Handicapped Children
  National Children's Bureau, 8 Wakley Street, London EC1V 7QE

This is an independently elected council established under the aegis of the National Children's Bureau. It provides an information service and a forum for discussion and action on all aspects of disability in childhood.

Wales Council for the Disabled
  Llys Ifor, Crescent Road, Caerphilly, Mid Glamorgan CF8 1XL

This is the co-ordinating body for voluntary and statutory organisations for the disabled in Wales. It provides information and advice on local amenities, including a guide for disabled holidaymakers.

PART THREE

The personal needs of physically handicapped people

12 Assessing the needs of physically handicapped people

In social services departments, the purpose of assessing the needs of physically handicapped clients is to bring to them the appropriate services which councils provide and to advise on other services that may be required. These can be services in terms of people, such as social workers or home-helps, or in terms of practical aid, such as the provision of aids to daily living, adaptations, holidays, day care, etc. An indirect purpose of assessment is to find out where there are gaps in services so that councils can be made aware of where provision will be required in the future.

The initial assessment may be carried out by a social worker or occupational therapist and will be aimed at detecting any difficulties which the person or his family are experiencing. It is essential that this assessment is as comprehensive as possible because what may be expressed as the only problem may cover many other difficulties. It may not be possible to assess someone fully at the first meeting, as time may be required to uncover some of the difficulties. It is as well to remember that difficulties which are only minor ones now may become insurmountable problems later on. If they are tackled in time one may help to maintain independence.

Many people who are experiencing a gradual deterioration in their physical condition may resign themselves to disability when, with help in the form of careful assessment, advice, aids and practice, they could find new ways of performing tasks independently. Others bitterly regret their inabilities and only give up their independence with a fight, marking off each successive failure as it happens: "This time last year I could do that without help." Likewise, a person's social environment may imperceptibly shrink until he is confined to

117

the four walls of his home with little motivation or energy to tackle the problem of trying to expand it again.

In carrying out an assessment, checklists may be useful in order to cover all aspects of daily life. The assessor should ask for movements and methods of doing things to be demonstrated where possible, rather than accepting a description from the client. In this way the assessment will be more useful and lead the way to selecting the most appropriate forms of help.

The following functional assessment is used by occupational therapists and is a useful guide to the kind of questions which need to be asked. (Functional assessment finds out the present level of personal competence from the disabled person's point of view.)

What can the person do for himself? For example, can he wash, dress and toilet himself, get in and out of bed, move about, get on and off chairs and up and down steps?

What does he want to be able to do? For example, does he feel he has anything to get up and get moving for?

What does he need to be able to do? For example, in his circumstances, to what extent does he need to budget and cook?

What does he need, to enable him to do these things?

(a) Can he be helped to understand and manage his situation?

(b) Can he develop the necessary skills? If so, how?

(c) How much practice does he need to achieve and maintain this skill and how should practice be graded?

(d) Can he be provided with help to increase his self-awareness, explore his conflicts and re-evaluate his abilities and performance – for example, so that he can acknowledge the reality of his situation?

(e) Does he need an aid? For eating, dressing, toilet or bath? For mobility? A walking aid or wheelchair? To control his environment? An automatic door opener, a full Possum (see Chapter 14)?

(f) Which model of the aid would be most appropriate?

(g) What training does he require to use his aid? Simple bath aids can be dangerous if used incorrectly and wheelchair living does not come naturally.

(*h*) Does his home need a structural alteration (which can be anything from a handrail to a bathroom extension)?

What activities give structure to his life now? And in the future?

(*a*) What hobbies, interests and social contacts does he have? How can he best incorporate these into his future lifestyle?

(*b*) Is it realistic for him to return to work? Or to seek alternative employment or sheltered employment?

Who is already involved? Family, professional workers, volunteers, others? And to what depth? Does his family need help to help him?

Who else offers the skills or services he needs to facilitate an adjustment? Nurse, physiotherapist, occupational therapist, social worker, home help, family aide, voluntary worker, etc?

The answers to these questions will help to build up a total picture of the handicapped person, his family and contacts.

A checklist covering different aspects of daily life might be constructed under the following headings, with an indication of areas of difficulty, where help is already given or needed.

Personal activities
Eating and drinking
Dressing and undressing
Washing
Shaving
Toilet
Combing hair
Cleaning teeth
Managing false teeth
Managing glasses
Managing hearing aid
Managing appliances, e.g. calipers, colostomy

Communication
Speaking
Reading
Writing
Use of telephone
Summoning help

119

General mobility indoors
Getting in and out of bed
Getting in and out of a chair
Walking
Wheelchair propulsion
Getting from room to room on the level
Going up and down steps and stairs
Getting on and off the toilet
Getting in and out of bath and shower
Getting to the front door

General mobility outside
Going in and out of the house at front door, back door
Walking outside (on rough ground)
Propelling wheelchair outside
Getting in and out of a car
Getting to and from neighbours, shops, etc.
Getting to work, school, other places

Domestic activities
Preparing food
Budgeting and managing diet
Laundry
General cleaning
Bed making

Family
Who helps, how much help is given and if there are
difficulties

Social contacts

Financial situation
If difficulties are experienced, what further benefits could be
claimed?

Leisure activities
At home and outside the home

Work
What are the prospects in the short and long term?

After an assessment of the current situation has been made,
areas of need emerge, very often in two groups: those which
must be tackled immediately for the sake of daily survival,

and those which can be considered as part of a planned programme of work with the person.

The remaining chapters in Part Three give information
related to the practical needs of physically handicapped people
and their families.

13 Looking after a disabled person

Social services workers in residential homes and in day centres are required to give help to physically handicapped clients who are dependent upon a considerable degree of physical help. Social workers and occupational therapists are called upon to support families with a severely disabled member who is not independent in daily living activities. The increasing trend towards home care projects, which maintain physically handicapped people in their own homes for as long as possible, means that different categories of home care attendants are being employed to work with people at home. All these staff need some understanding of methods of physically handling clients to enable them either to do it themselves or to advise others.

The presence of handicap in a member of the family often produces a subtle or even overt change in the established roles of the family members. Roles have evolved partly as a result of the tasks undertaken by each member. The husband, for instance, may do the garden, minor repairs and decorating, earn the income, pay the bills and run and look after the car. His wife takes care of the housework, shopping and cooking, looks after the children and does the washing and ironing. If the man becomes severely physically handicapped his wife may have to take on his role-tasks – earning the income, repairing and decorating the house, and so on. But at the same time she still has her own tasks, *plus* physically looking after her husband as well. If the woman becomes severely physically handicapped then it is the husband who must take on his wife's tasks of housework, shopping, children, etc., *as well as* looking after his wife.

The additional physical strain can be immense and there is

the added psychological strain of coping with a partner who is, perhaps, unable to adjust to disability and who may be suffering depression and frustration. The older the children are the more they may be able to help, but usually the greatest burden falls upon one person, the marriage partner. Similar problems can occur where the family consists of an elderly disabled parent, or parents, and their adult son or daughter. Change of role may happen suddenly in the case of sudden disability, or very slowly as a person's condition deteriorates.

The Attendance Allowance acknowledges financially the difficulties of looking after a severely disabled person at home, and is wisely paid to the disabled person himself, which does allow him some sense of being able to provide financial recompense for the added work he knows he makes. There is a great need for skilled counselling in such situations for it is often the quality of relationships which is tested and families may need to work hard at staying together. However, it is the physical tasks themselves which can become so tiring that they stretch relationships to their bounds. If some of these tasks can be made easier then people can often learn to cope.

Management in bed

If a person is to spend most of his time in bed, it is often best for the bed to be placed close to the hub of the house rather than tucked away upstairs. This enables the disabled person to take part in family life and at the same time avoids the need for his partner to run up and down stairs to him throughout the day.

A sit-up bed (Fig. 2), that is one which is in three parts and can be converted from a horizontal position to a sit-up position, will enable him to change position for meals, watching television and conversing with visitors and lie down easily when he is tired and wants to rest. Several different types of sit-up beds are available and are usually operated electrically with the minimum of effort. Often the disabled person himself can manage to operate the switch.

If this kind of bed is not available and the person uses an ordinary bed, then an over-bed handle may be helpful to enable him to pull himself up to a sitting position. A back rest will also be required to support him when sitting up. Lifting a person up in the bed can be very difficult for one helper when the disabled person cannot help himself at all

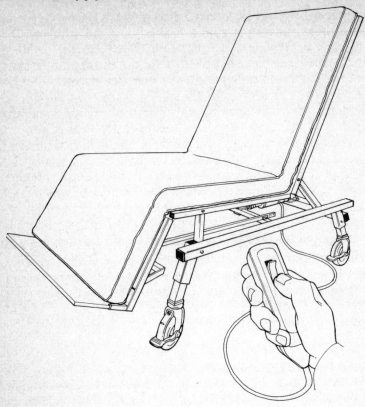

Fig. 2 Sit-up bed

and often the partner must wait until there is someone there to help her. This is where the sit-up bed is particularly useful.

Prevention of pressure sores

Normally we are constantly moving our bodies to prevent the discomfort of being too long in one position. Moving is so unconscious an action that it is only when we are ill and confined to bed that we realise how quickly skin can get red and sore. It need only be a matter of a few days before this soreness develops, particularly on the buttocks, the lower part of the back and the heels. There are two reasons for pressure sore places; firstly there is the constant pressure of the body weight on the bed, increased by the weight of the bedclothes, and secondly the sluggishness of circulation due to lack of muscle work pumping the blood back to the heart. The pressure can be relieved in various ways.

1. Regularly turning the person from one side to the other every few hours will help, as he is not then lying on the same part of his body all the time.
2. An alternating pressure, or ripple, mattress can be used. This device is operated electrically and is made up of two sets of tubes lying side by side across the width of the mattress which inflate alternately every few minutes, giving a ripple effect.
3. Synthetic sheepskin bedsheets are now available which reduce the effect of pressure, because they are both springy and allow the passage of air between the fibres.

Regular treatment of the skin over pressure points is necessary, whichever of the above methods is used. The skin needs to be kept clean by washing regularly with soap and water and then dried thoroughly. A little cream rubbed into the skin will then prevent it from becoming dry and cracked and will keep it supple.

If the person is incontinent, extra care should be taken, because urine can irritate the skin and constant wetness can cause sores. Bed pads need frequent changing and the use of special bedsheets for incontinence is recommended (see Chapter 17).

Toileting

If the person needs the toilet frequently and is unable to be got out of bed on to a commode, there are various methods of toileting in bed.

1. A bedpan can be used if the person can lift himself up or be lifted up to sit on it. Anyone who has been in hospital and had to use a bedpan will understand how difficult it is to balance upon. Sometimes the person can be propped up on it but many people find it difficult, especially for a bowel action.
2. A portable male or female urinal is convenient to use in bed and it is best if the person can sit up a little to allow for downward drainage into the vessel.
3. An Easinurse mattress is another alternative. This is a mattress with a hole cut out to take an ordinary bedpan,

which is placed underneath, resting on the base of the bed. The person needs to be able to position himself so that he can empty over the hole. Sheets are supplied with this mattress which are specially cut out. One is of plastic and incorporates a drainage funnel, the other is cotton and goes over the top. An Easinurse cushion on the same principle is made to fit in an armchair.

It is desirable for the person to be got out of bed to use the commode sometimes during the day. This will be best when the bowels are to be moved, as sitting up with the feet firmly on the floor is a much better position. Constipation can be a serious problem with bed-bound people and it may be avoided in this way. A district nurse will usually be available for such a patient and will attend to the problem of constipation should it arise. If necessary she may have to perform a manual evacuation of the bowels.

Lifting a person on or off bed/chair/commode/toilet

Lifting is a difficult task for one person and requires some study as to the most efficient method to employ. A nurse, physiotherapist or occupational therapist will be able to advise in individual cases on the best way to manage different people. It is absolutely essential that the correct method is chosen and learned because damage can be done to the lifter's back in seconds which will last for a lifetime. It is simply not worth the risk to lift wrongly and without thought.*

There will always be occasions when the helper feels she has to lift quickly in a crisis situation and then there is a risk of twisting the spine, which, together with the strain of the weight, can cause injury to the back. Therefore, the following points should always be remembered. If time is taken to consider each point in turn then the exercise should be performed in the most satisfactory ways for both lifter and lifted.

1. Make sure the task is within your capabilities (given the

---

* Approved methods of lifting handicapped people are described and illustrated in the book *Handling the Handicapped*, published by Woodhead-Faulkner in association with the Chartered Society of Physiotherapy. A film based on the book, 'Moving and Lifting the Disabled Person,' is available for hire or purchase from the same publishers, and is excellent for training purposes.

situation, equipment, etc.). If it is not, then arrange for help (other staff, neighbours, and so on).

2. Tell the disabled person what you are about to do and gain his co-operation.
3. Place all equipment and furniture so that the minimum amount of manoeuvring will be required. Make sure that there are no hazards in the way and that brakes are engaged on movable pieces such as the wheelchair.
4. Again, give the disabled person instructions as to how he can help. If there are handrails or a large solid piece of furniture nearby which he might hold onto while standing, then this may help.
5. In a deliberate and unhurried way, move.
6. Lift from the knees and hips, keeping the back straight. Use your whole body to brace yourself against anything firm.

Hoists

Various types of hoists are available to lift a disabled person. The choice of hoist will depend upon how much space is available in the room and on the person who will operate it. The choice of slings will depend upon what kind of support the disabled person requires. The choice of both hoist and slings is best made in consultation with a nurse, occupational therapist or physiotherapist, or with staff in hospitals.

Bathing, showering and washing hair

A complete wash in bed is a service performed by community nurses for many disabled people at home who may be bed-bound and unable to use the bath. However, most people much prefer the refreshing feeling of washing all over by soaking themselves in water and indeed a soak in a hot bath can be very beneficial to those who suffer from stiff and painful joints and, particularly, from back pain.

The use of an Autolift bath hoist or overhead track bath hoist, described in Chapter 15, can assist the helper to lift the person into the bath with a minimum of effort. Alternatively, the bath may be removed and replaced by a level-access shower to enable a shower chair to be wheeled into the shower area. This adaptation is only suitable where the bathroom is on the ground floor, the floor being tiled to slope down to the drainage point. An extra-long shower curtain tucked in at the bottom will prevent water from escaping on to the rest of the bathroom floor.

If the person is unable to wash himself under the shower, there is always the difficulty of the helper washing him without getting drenched herself! This takes some practice and most people need to find their own way of accomplishing it. It is often best to take off one's shoes and stockings and put on a long plastic apron. Sleeves are rolled up as high as possible. Once the person has become thoroughly wet by having the shower played over him, then the hose can be laid on the ground or turned away from the body and the person soaped all over. There are many preparations of soap especially designed for showering and some of these come in a liquid form. Once the soaping is completed then the person can be rinsed.

The choice of a shower chair will depend on the support needed by the disabled person, on whether he can propel himself in the chair and on whether the shower chair is to be taken from bedroom into shower room, in which case the door width will have to be taken into account. Some shower chairs incorporate a toilet seat to enable the person to be wheeled over the toilet pan either before or after the shower. Some of these shower chairs also have a fitting to take a bedpan underneath the toilet aperture.

There is often more room in the bedroom to transfer the person into the shower chair. Once in the chair, undressed, with a dressing gown wrapped round, he can be wheeled into the shower area, uncovered and showered. On the return journey it may be warmer to dry and dress in the bedroom.

Hair can be washed in the shower, or with a shower fitting on the bath taps. If, however, a person is bed-bound for a long time, there is a hair-washing basin designed for use in bed. This aid has a neck rest and drains into a bucket placed beside the bed. It is important to realise how much fresher a person can feel when he has had his hair washed and dried. This is especially true with women, as is the need to keep the face and hands fresh. A little cream on the face will prevent dry and flaky skin and elderly women who may grow excessive facial hair should be regularly shaved. All in all, the appearance is just as important for a severely disabled person as for anyone else, if not more so.

Dressing and feeding are dealt with in the next chapter; it

is useful to remember that if the person is completely dependent, then these activities assume a profound importance to him and need to be undertaken in an unhurried and caring way.

Interest activities

For the person confined to bed or wheelchair, unable to do much for himself, the days can seem long and boring. Television and radio can help and reading should not be abandoned if it is of interest. A daily paper or magazine can be supported on one of the aids available for use either flat in bed or sitting up. Large print books are popular and a good directional reading light on the print is beneficial and prevents eye strain and fatigue.

Other interests and hobbies should be investigated to see if they can still be pursued or new ones within the capabilities of the person introduced. Handicraft instructors are employed in most social services departments to provide activity for people in their own homes and these staff are trained to adapt crafts to a person's limited abilities.

Families with a disabled member usually benefit from a short break from caring and attendance at a day centre for the disabled person sometime during the week will release the caring relative to visit friends, catch up on jobs or simply relax in whichever way she chooses. Similarly, an annual holiday can be arranged for the disabled person, either alone or with his family, at one of the holiday places run for dependent disabled people. Both disabled person and caring relative will then get a well-earned rest. It is easier to continue when there is the chance of a break to look forward to; however fond the couple may be of each other, both looking after and being looked after can be a relentless job.

14 Personal activities and communication

All the activities considered in this chapter are those which are most personal to everyone. Four main areas of activity and their associated problems are examined: eating and drinking, dressing, personal toilet and communication. Inability to perform them reduces the person to a very dependent, childhood level and, therefore, whatever the cause of the disability an endeavour should be made to find some way whereby the person can care for himself without having to ask for too much help.

Eating and drinking

From childhood, eating and drinking are the first activities which assert personal independence. When an adult has to be fed he regresses functionally to a childhood level of dependence.

Chewing and swallowing are the earliest movements a child learns; then he learns to carry the food from the plate to his mouth and later to cut up the food upon the plate. Drinking starts with sucking and swallowing and then carrying the liquid container to the mouth, without spilling, and pouring in. Throughout his training the child is taught to eat and drink in a socially acceptable way, for this is one activity which is essential for "good" social contact. Different disabilities impose different restrictions on each stage of these activities.

Problem: The person is unable to cut up his food but can carry it to his mouth and eat

People with weak or arthritic hands find it difficult to grip the handle of a knife or fork firmly enough to exert pressure on the food to cut it. If cutlery handles are enlarged then gripping is made easier. This can be done in several ways. Large-handled cutlery can be bought from specialised firms and is attractive and presentable in company. Usually the enlarged handles are made of plastic; some common styles are shown in Fig. 3.

Fig. 3 Types of large-handled cutlery

For quick adaptation of the person's own cutlery, a rubber tubing is manufactured in lengths which can be cut up to fit on any piece of cutlery (Fig. 4). This is commonly called Rubbazote tubing and comes in differing sizes of bore. It can also be used for "thickening" pens and pencils. Other disabilities which cause weakness of grip are stroke, Parkinson's disease, multiple sclerosis and spinal injuries.

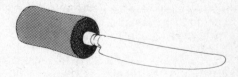

Fig. 4 An ordinary knife fitted with Rubbazote tubing

Sometimes, if the hands are very weak, there will need to be a strap attachment to the cutlery which can actually strap round the hand. Then the cutting movement can be made by moving the arm backwards and forwards. However, this is very difficult to control and is more successful for scooping up food with a spoon. Then help will be required to cut the food.

Problem: The person cannot lift the utensil and carry it to his mouth

If the wrist is weak, as well as the grip, the combined weight of spoon and food will often be too much to lift off the plate. Then very light cutlery is required (with a thickened handle). The arm may be rested on the table and the head brought closer to the plate. This method of eating is also useful where there is gross tremor and the journey from plate to mouth results in spilling. With practice, eating this way can become quite neat.

Cups containing liquid can be heavy to lift and easy to spill. A light plastic beaker is made, with two long handles, which can be useful (Fig. 5). The whole hand can be passed right through the handle to grip round the beaker. Obviously, a half-filled beaker is safer and avoids spilling.

Fig. 5 Long-handled plastic beakers. The model on the left is lighter, but that on the right more versatile

When rheumatoid arthritis affects the neck, shoulders, elbows and wrists it is usually difficult for the person to reach his mouth with the spoon or fork. The arms are stiff and will not bend up to the head. Some long-handled cutlery is made to help bridge the gap. It needs to be light and it takes some skill to manoeuvre the food into the mouth. Sometimes the stem of the spoon needs to be angled slightly just behind the bowl to make it easier to enter the mouth at an angle (Fig. 6). Many people become extremely proficient at using long-handled tools, so many activities being centred around the head and hands.

Fig. 6 Long-handled spoon with angled stem (left- and right-handed versions)

Problem: Chewing and swallowing is impaired in some way

This can happen after a stroke, when the muscles of the mouth may be affected. At first minced and sloppy foods may be given but these may become monotonous and unappetising for the person and the ultimate aim should be to re-educate the muscles of mastication. A speech therapist will help to retrain the person by teaching various exercises both with and without the use of food.

If the person is disabled enough to need to be fed, then a relaxed and easy approach is required in order to prevent an increase in anxiety, which can lead to choking while swallowing. Feeding should take place in an unhurried way, with occasional pauses to allow all the food to be cleared from the mouth before the next mouthful. It is very important to ensure that the food is kept warm and appetising. Plates such as that illustrated in Fig. 7 have a sealed container in the bottom for boiling water, which will help to keep the plate, and hence the food, hot. An electric hotplate might be another alternative.

Frequent sips of water or squash will help to wash the food down. Never rush a person eating, or make him feel that feeding him is a trouble. He is already feeling totally dependent upon you. The same person feeding him regularly will help you both to build up a relationship whereby he will get

Fig. 7 The base of this type of plate holds a sealed container, which is filled with boiling water through the nozzle shown

his food in the order in which he wants to eat it, at the speed set by him. Small signs will tell you when he is ready for the next mouthful without him having to say "Ready" or "Greens next"!

Problem: Onehandedness

The fascinating thing about hands is that they work as a pair. One hand is usually dominant, i.e. it directs the work, but the other hand is of equal importance because it holds and steadies. Practically everything we do with our pair of hands is done in this way – the one hand holds, the other acts. So it is with eating: the fork hand holds while the knife hand cuts, the fork is held still while the knife hand pushes the food on to it, and the fork hand holds still whilst the spoon hand scoops up the food against it. When the use of one hand is lost, usually after a stroke, then the remaining hand has to be the active one (whether it was the dominant hand or not).

However, the holding and steadying function of the other hand is missed and something else must take its place.

A Dycem mat (see Fig. 8) will keep the plate from slipping away on the table. This mat is made of a plastic with an apparently sticky surface.

The edges of a deep bowl will act as a pusher, up against which food can be tipped into the bowl of the spoon. There is a shaped plate manufactured in the Manoy tableware range which incorporates a steep edge into its design, against which food can be pushed (Fig. 8).

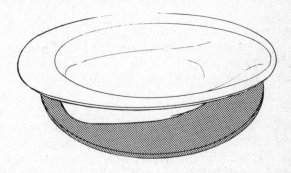

Fig. 8 Specially shaped Manoy plate standing on a Dycem mat

A knife with a curved cutting edge, rather like a cheese knife, is available, which with a rolling motion can be used to cut up food without pushing it back and forth across the plate (Fig. 9).

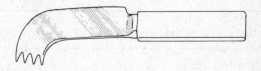

Fig. 9 Nelson knife with curved cutting edge

A boiled egg can be impossible to manage one-handed without a plastic suction egg cup which grips the plate below and the egg in its bowl (Fig. 10).

When someone is having difficulty with eating and drinking for any of the above reasons, it is useful to have available a

135

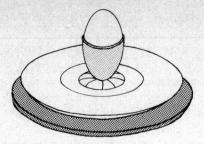

Fig. 10 This plastic suction egg cup grips both the egg and the plate below. The plate here stands on a Dycem mat for added grip

full range of assorted utensils for him to try out. After all, everyone has his own individual ways and preferences and it can be depressing and frustrating not to find some way of being independent in eating and drinking.

Dressing

The activities of dressing and undressing demand some of the most complicated bodily movements which an individual will ever have to perform. The hands roam over and around the whole body which balances, bends and postures in order to be covered from neck to toe. Added to this there is the necessity to look neat, sleek and clean. Everyone feels good when they are nicely dressed and know that they look good. This, however, can be difficult to achieve when the person is alone and cannot put all his clothes on properly. Other people can never quite dress him as well as he can himself; there may be an irritating wrinkle here or a certain tightness there. So it is desirable for him to be independent in dressing if possible.

The first consideration is the choice of clothes which will make it easier to dress independently, or to adapt clothes so that they are easier to manage. Modern fabrics which are soft and stretchy, but hang well and are crease resistant, help disabled people to look smart. They are also much easier to wash and dry and they do not need ironing.

Most people have their own routine for putting on their clothes, which may need altering when they become disabled. Some clothes go over the feet and are pulled up, others go over the head and arms and are pulled down, and there are those where the arms go through and they are wrapped round. Fastenings present the final problem.

136

Problem: The person is unable to get clothes over the feet and pull them up

Arthritis, particularly of hips and knees, obesity and diseases of the chest and heart are among those which make it difficult to bend down to the feet. People with back injuries find it impossible to bend, and some people with eye complaints are advised not to bend down. Sitting down can seem to bring the feet closer to the hands but, even then, putting on knickers, pants, stockings, socks and shoes can be a problem: the reach is just not long enough. When this is the case often an aid is required to extend the reach of the arms.

A stocking aid or gutter has been invented to enable the person to put on stockings or socks neatly, with the toe and heel in the right place (Fig. 11). It is basically a very simple aid (all the best ones are), just a piece of flat Perspex which can be bent round and inserted into the toe of the sock or stocking, which is first gathered up. The gutter is dropped to the floor by means of the long tapes attached to the top and the foot is inserted into the gutter, which is then pulled up the leg, leaving the stocking gradually as it goes.

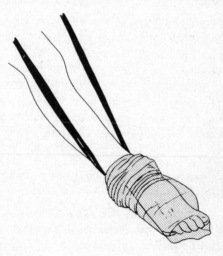

Fig. 11 Stocking aid

Knickers and pants can often be managed by using a pick-up stick (like the Helping Hand). This holds first one leg open whilst the foot is pushed through, then the other leg likewise, and then the pants are pulled up. Trousers are usually easier, because they are longer pieces of clothing, but it is important to put the more severely affected leg in first whilst there is still room for manoeuvre, and then the better leg afterwards. Standing up to pull these clothes up to the waist can be a problem, especially if the balance is poor and the person needs two hands to support himself. Also, as he stands up, the trousers are inclined to drop down so that he must sit down to retrieve them, and so it can go on! Wearing braces may help. If the person can get his trousers up far enough while he is sitting down, to wriggle the waist band under his bottom, then he might be able to hook the braces over his arms and so secure the trousers whilst he stands up.

Shoes can present the worst problem unless they are of the loose, slip-on variety, but these will be less likely to support his feet for walking. Slippers are the easiest of all but give no support. A long-handled shoe horn can prove useful together with a piece of furniture or wall to push the toe of the shoe against as the foot is pushed forward into it.

Shoes with calipers attached (Fig. 12) are very difficult to manage and it is easier to slip the caliper out of the heel-box, put the shoe on and then slip the caliper back into its heel-box and pull the top part back to clasp it round the calf. Usually calipers have a strong spring at the bottom which is designed to counter foot drop, so that the iron has to be pulled firmly back against the spring to get the upper band round the calf.

Elastic shoe laces can be purchased which need not be untied but which will give when the foot is pushed into the shoe.

Problem: The person has difficulty in getting clothes over the head and pulling them down

Any disability which affects the arms makes it difficult both to lift clothes over the head and to push the arms into armholes so that they can be pulled down over the top half of the body. Vests, jumpers and dresses have to be put on this way when they do not open right down the front. It is always best to put the head in first, then the more disabled arm and then the better arm last of all. Obviously, clothes which stretch are easier than those which do not and loose clothes are better than those which are of a tighter fit. Pulling off these garments

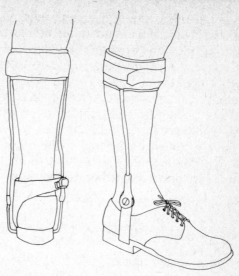

Fig. 12 Caliper and shoe

can also be difficult and some people find the easiest way is to grasp the back of the collar firmly with the better arm and pull the garment forward over the head.

There are no really good aids to help with this activity and the person will very much rely on the design of his clothes. Some people choose as many clothes as they can which will fasten right down the front and therefore do not need pulling on over the head.

Problem: *The person has difficulty in putting on clothes which wrap round*

The most difficult garments to put on are usually those which are termed "foundation" garments. Many women stop wearing brassieres and corsets when they become disabled simply because they are so difficult to put on. This is regrettable, because women who are used to supporting their bust and holding in their waist and tummy often feel very uncomfortable when these garments are left off. Corsets are often medically prescribed to support the back and are therefore necessarily tight.

Brassieres which fasten in the front are easier than those which fasten at the back. Back-fastening bras can be managed by wrapping them round, fastening them in front, and then pulling the whole bra round until the cups are at the front and putting the arms through the straps.

Corsets may need to be adapted to different fastenings. Instead of the row of tiny hooks and eyes, larger hooks and eyes might be sewn-on, or D-rings and Velcro (Fig. 13). Velcro is a modern fastening consisting of two pieces of nylon ribbon. One piece of ribbon is covered with a tiny, hook-like pile which is rough to the touch, the other piece is covered with a tiny eye-like pile which is soft to the touch. When the two pieces are pressed together they stick firmly to each other.

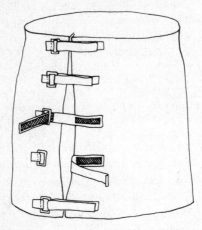

Fig. 13 Corset with Velcro fastenings

Other clothes which wrap round are shirts, blouses, cardigans, jackets and button-through dresses. When these clothes are lightweight they are easier to put on than those which pull over the head, but heavier jackets and coats can be a problem. Often the only solution for people with stiff and weak arms is to get help to put on heavy coats or jackets, or to avoid wearing them at all and stick to thicker cardigans, capes and ponchos.

Problem: Fastenings

So many clothing fasteners are very small and prove difficult for arthritic fingers, fingers which have lost fine sensation and weak hands. Often it is better to adapt fastenings on garments so that the person can manage them without help.

Buttons and button holes can be replaced by small Velcro patches, zips by a Velcro strip. Sometimes zips can be managed by threading a keyring or a length of cord through the hole in the zip handle. Then the fingers can more easily pull on the larger loop and draw the zip up or down. Large hooks and eyes, of the type used for fastening waistbands, are also useful.

Problem: Onehandedness

After suffering a stroke the person with a one-sided paralysis (hemiplegia) may lose the perception of his body image. Not only has he lost the function of his hand, arm and leg but he may be unable to dress himself because he does not know where his limbs are in space. This disability presents serious problems in dressing and undressing, problems which usually require the skilled work of an occupational therapist to help him to re-educate his perception, if this is at all possible.

If the perception of body image and position sense are not disrupted, then the person will be able to make a good attempt at dressing. He will need to dress his affected side first with each garment, putting his unaffected side in after. For example, he will feed the shirtsleeve on to his affected arm, pulling it right up to the shoulder, and then, grasping the collar, he will pull the shirt round behind his neck and reaching back for the other sleeve, push his unaffected arm into it. Finally he will bring the front fastenings together.

Re-education of dressing can be a slow process at first, but gradually, after one or two tries *without help*, the disabled person will begin to get the hang of it and become quicker. The sense of achievement can be very rewarding and may encourage him to go on seeking independence in other personal activities.

Personal toilet

Washing face and hands, shaving and cleaning the teeth are activities which most people, unless very severely disabled, can perform providing that one hand can be brought up to the face. They are activities which should always be carried out by the person himself if he is capable of them. Even if he cannot get his hand right up to his face, as in the case of rheumatoid arthritis affecting elbows and shoulders, he may be able to use a sponge on a long handle for washing.

141

Electric razors and electric toothbrushes are invaluable for disabled people, as they take the hard work out of shaving and cleaning teeth.

Combing the hair can be a little more difficult, as it requires getting round to the back of the head, and tangled hair can provide some resistance to the comb. A good brush or a long-handled comb may be better. The latter is available as a ready-made aid, but can easily be made from a piece of drilled dowelling and a tail comb, as shown in Fig. 14.

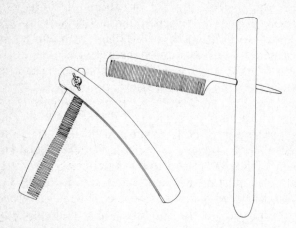

Fig. 14 Long-handled combs

Adjusting false teeth, glasses and hearing aids can be problematic to the person with rheumatoid arthritis but given encouragement people often find their own solutions.

Blowing the nose may also be difficult and there is an aid which is like a small pair of tongs which holds a handkerchief or tissue to the nose if the hands cannot reach.

Using the lavatory is probably the most worrying personal activity for those disabled people who find it a problem and this is considered in more detail in the next chapter.

Communication

In Chapter 3 we looked at some speech problems associated with strokes, with simple hints on how to approach the person. Other disabilities can cause a breakdown in intelligible speech and a speech therapist should always be consulted for advice. If the person is not going to be referred for speech therapy then it should be possible for the social worker to obtain advice herself. Most speech therapists will be only too pleased to discuss the problem over the telephone or will arrange to meet you and your client to advise.

Aids to communication, such as word boards or picture charts, are best introduced on the advice of the speech therapist. Where a family is having particular problems it is advisable to ask the family doctor to refer them for a speech therapist's advice. Nothing can damage family relationships quicker than non-communication. Some disabled people who do not have intelligible speech communicate using either a typewriter or a lightwriter. A lightwriter is similar in appearance to a pocket calculator, with the letters of the alphabet in place of numbers. As words are spelled out they can be read in light letters on the display screen. Other people may be proficient with a letter board. This is simply a small board bearing the letters of the alphabet, the numbers 1 to 10 and "YES/NO/THANK YOU". The user spells out his message by pointing.

Possum Environmental Control Systems, such as PSU3, allow a severely disabled person to communicate and to manipulate his environment. The person operates the system by using whatever residual movement he has. If he can move a hand he can use a light touch manual control switch, and if he cannot, he can be supplied with a suck–blow mechanism or a pressure pad mounted so that he can use it with head, elbow, foot or whatever limb he can move.

Using the PSU3 Environmental Control System, the disabled person can operate an alarm and intercoms, open the front door, turn on the light, dial a telephone number and operate his radio, television or tape recorder. He does this by watching a light move across the control board and by stopping it at the service he wishes to use (see Fig. 15). In the same manner, a person with no speech can use the Possum Typewriter Control System to operate a keyboard. This allows him to communicate with family and friends and opens the door to education and employment.

Possum Environmental Control and Typewriter Systems can be supplied by the DHSS. Referral should be made by the family doctor or hospital specialist to the Area or Regional Health Authority. A special assessment is then made in the person's own home by an assessor who is also a doctor. If he

Fig. 15 Possum indicator board, showing an example of the range of activities which can be controlled by this system

recommends a Possum, then Possum Controls Ltd send a trained occupational therapist to advise upon the exact equipment needed. Social services departments are usually asked to arrange for preparatory electrical work to be carried out prior to the installation and the cost is borne by the DHSS. Where delays are encountered with an application, Possum Controls Ltd can often expedite matters if they are informed.

The telephone, of course, is an important communication aid for many disabled people and helps to combat the isolation that disability can cause. The Post Office manufactures a variety of telephone aids, including amplified hand sets, push-button dials, lightweight handsets and handset stands. There is, however, an increased rental for these aids. When installing a telephone it is important to site it where it is going to be accessible. Often an extension is also required, so that the person can have one receiver in the living room and another beside the bed. For ambulant clients, one receiver on a long lead, which can be taken from room to room, may be manageable but care should be taken that the telephone cable is not a hazard to walking.

The ability to call for help in an emergency is vital to some people, especially those who live alone, and there is a variety of alarm systems on the market. However, the best alarm is always the one which alerts a known person rather than rings out to all and sundry, relying on a passer-by to answer the alarm call. If someone needs an alarm system a neighbour might be approached as the receiver of the signal. If there is no one to take on this role it is rather pointless to install the alarm. It could also be dangerous, as it is not unknown for unscrupulous people to answer the alarm and then to take advantage of the helplessness of the disabled person.

15 General mobility indoors

In order to perform most daily living activities independently, a person must be reasonably mobile and able to move from room to room in his house. Some activities have to be performed regularly and may present problems to the physically handicapped person. Below are listed some particular problems with possible solutions.

To assess the person's problems in mobility it will be necessary to ask him to demonstrate. A verbal description is often not sufficient when seeking a solution. The more complex mobility problems will require assessment by an occupational therapist.

Going to the lavatory

Problem: The person can get to the toilet but is unsteady when getting on or off or is unstable when seated

A toilet frame (Fig. 16), or handrails on the walls on either side of the toilet, will help a person with this problem provided that they are within the person's reach.

Problem: The person has difficulty in getting down to the toilet and rising after use

A toilet frame with seat (Fig. 17), or a raised toilet seat which fits to the toilet pan, could be helpful as it will raise the height of the toilet pan. If a raised toilet seat is supplied, then handrails may also be required on the walls of the toilet cubicle, provided that these are well within reach.

Fig. 16 Simple toilet frame

Problem: *The person cannot manage his clothes*

Light fabrics which slip easily are easier for women to manage.
Skirts can be tucked into waistbands and open-crutch pants
or those with a flap can be useful.

For men, trousers worn with braces may be easier to manage than a belt, as the trousers can be easier to retrieve from
around the ankles. Many disabled men who cannot stand
unaided find sitting down to urinate is more satisfactory (although it can take some getting used to!).

Problem: *The person cannot clean himself*

Some people find it difficult to reach round or underneath to
clean themselves. Where this is an impossibility, the installation of a Closomat or Medic-loo toilet which incorporates a
washing/drying mechanism is an invaluable aid to independence. This is a most intimate activity and any help is usually

147

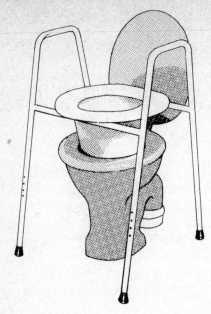

Fig. 17 Toilet frame with raised seat

unacceptable. A person's dignity is preserved if this task can be performed in private.

Problem: The person cannot get to the toilet

The location of the toilet may make it inaccessible to a person with impaired mobility. There is a variety of possible solutions, which will depend on the structure of the house, the person's lifestyle and the resources of the local authority. The table below sets out some of the usual problems of location and suggests various possible solutions.

Problem	*Solution*
1. The toilet is situated outside in the garden	Turn toilet cubicle to open indoors Build an indoor toilet Install commode or chemical toilet indoors
2. Toilet is inside but steps and stairs are involved in getting to it	Make level access if possible Install stairlift Install commode or chemical toilet

3. The doorway is too narrow for walking aid or wheelchair

Widen doorway if possible
Install handrails to enable walking in without aids
Install commode or chemical toilet

4. Toilet door is wide enough but opens the wrong way so that person cannot get in

Rehang door to open the other way
Fit sliding door if possible

Using the bathroom

Some of the most regular problems which occur are those involving bathing. Only the most able-bodied, it would seem, are capable of using the bath totally unaided. Immediately we begin to feel our age, and get a little stiffer or a little tired, we have to have our wits about us when entering or getting out of the bath. It would seem to be a combination of water, the naked body and the slippery surface of baths which makes this activity rather precarious. We would like to see a handrail on the wall as a standard fitting beside baths. Some modern baths do, however, have hand grips incorporated into the sides.

Problem: The person can get into the bath but cannot sit down without help

A bath seat which wedges in the bath with the seat about 6 inches from the bottom will help, as the person does not have to get right down on the bottom of the bath. This, together with a non-slip bath mat and a handrail on the wall (Fig. 18), will solve this problem in most cases.

Problem: The person cannot get into the bath but can lift his legs up to a horizontal position

A bath board placed across the top of the bath (Fig. 19) will enable the person to sit down on it and lift first one leg and then the other over the bath rim. An L-shaped handrail on the wall gives support both for holding on while lifting the legs and for pulling the bottom across the board. A bath seat and bath mat will then enable the person to get down into the water.

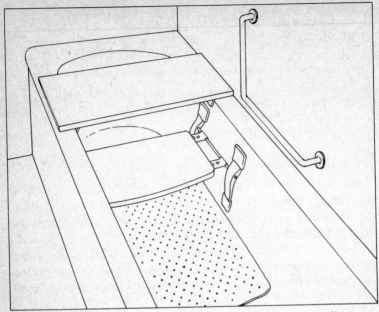

Fig. 18 A bath with wall-mounted handrail, bath seat and non-slip mat

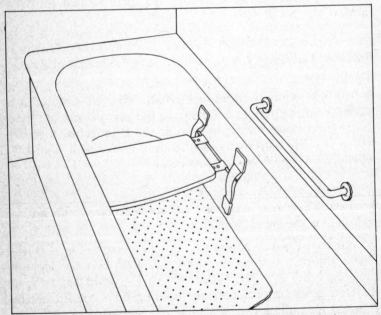

Fig. 19 A bath board in position, used in conjunction with a bath seat, handrail and mat

Problem: Wall-mounted rails are unsuitable because the person has difficulty in raising his arms sideways

A safety rail fitted to the taps will provide support for the person who can reach forward to pull himself up or let himself gently down. These are made for both straight taps and corner taps (Fig. 20). Again, these would usually be provided together with a bath seat and always with a bath mat if the person does not already have one.

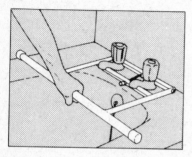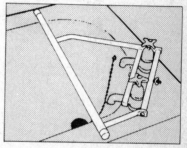

Fig. 20 Safety rail fitted to the bath taps. Models are available both for taps at the end of the bath and for those mounted in one corner

Problem: The person can get into the bath but cannot sit down, even with the provision of bath aids

The solution to this problem is to provide a shower and shower curtain so that the person can stand up and shower. Sometimes, if there is a large enough head of water (that is, the water pressure is strong enough), an ordinary shower attachment to the taps is adequate. In many cases, however, there is insufficient water pressure when the shower attachment is lifted up to shoulder height, or the water temperature is difficult to control and there is a danger of scalding. Then it is advisable to fit one of the compact wall-mounted shower fittings with its own instant, thermostatically controlled water heater. The electric type (e.g. Heatrae) is by far the most reliable and, although electric, is reasonably cheap to run, because a shower uses a fraction of the amount of water needed for a bath.

Problem: The person cannot get into the bath

For the person confined to a wheelchair because of paralysis or extreme stiffness or weakness, getting into a bath is virtually an impossibility without the use of more sophisticated aids. Two types of bath hoist, which lift the person bodily in and out of the bath, are commonly supplied for domestic use. One is floor-standing and the other is mounted on the ceiling on a running track.

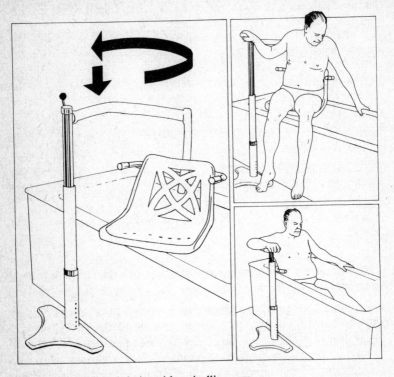

Fig. 21 Autolift bath hoist with swivelling seat

The Autolift bath hoist (Fig. 21) is a useful piece of equipment where there is space in the bathroom to use it. The hoist swivels round outside the bath, where the person is transferred onto the seat, and the seat is raised by means of a handle at the top of the column, swivelled round over the bath and then lowered into the water. The Autolift can be stored in the bath when not in use.

The overhead hoist is used with slings, placed around the body while the person is sitting in his wheelchair. The person is then raised up from the wheelchair, the hoist is drawn across an overhead track until he is suspended directly over the bath, and he is then lowered into the water. The advantage of the hoist is that it is stored out of the way, up near the ceiling, but two slings are required because they become wet and have to be dried. Then they must be removed from under the person when he comes out of the bath and is back in the wheelchair. An electric overhead track hoist is illustrated in Fig. 30, p. 174.

An alternative solution for people who cannot get into the bath is the provision of a shower either separately or in place of the existing bath, as described in the previous section.

When considering the problems of bathing it is advisable to discuss them with an occupational therapist, who will have experience in assessing the best method of tackling them given the existing disability.

Problem: The bathroom is inaccessible to the disabled person.

The location of the bathroom may make it inaccessible and possible problems and solutions are set out below.

Problem	*Solution*
1. Bathroom is inaccessible because there are steps and stairs involved	Make level access if possible Install stairslift Install shower cabinet in an accessible room
2. Bathroom door is too narrow for walking aid or wheelchair	Widen doorway if possible Install handrails to enable walking in without aids Install shower cabinet in an accessible room
3. There is not enough room in the bathroom to manoeuvre	Rehang bathroom door to open outwards Fit sliding door if possible Install sit-up bath or shower cabinet in place of existing bath

Steps and stairs

Many disabling conditions prevent people from climbing steps and stairs. This is because the whole body weight is being lifted up on one leg with each step climbed. Similarly, coming down the steps, the body weight is lowered down each step by one leg. The leading leg carries the weight up the step, the following leg carries the weight down the step. Thus, people are taught to lead up with the "good" leg and lead down with the "bad" leg.

Handrails on both sides of the steps or stairs will help the person to support his body weight and lift himself using his arms as well as his legs. Rails need to be stout, at least 1½ inches in diameter, circular in cross section and preferably made of wood. They need to be securely fixed to the wall. A length of handrail should extend at least a foot past the top and bottom step to allow for reach.

When stairs become too difficult to climb to make the effort involved worth while, then a stairslift should be considered as an alternative, to make both floors of the house accessible. This is an electrically operated chair which runs up the stairs on a track. An occupational therapist is usually the best person to assess for the type of stairslift which will be most suitable for both the client and the house. Platform stairslifts, which will carry a standing person or a wheelchair upstairs, are also available or a vertical lift may be considered. A simpler solution to the problem of stairs is for the person to resign himself to living on one level and to bring his bed downstairs. This solution is often preferred by very elderly folk who are not always able to accept, or use, mechanical equipment.

The bedroom

Getting in and out of bed and moving about in the bed can present difficulties to physically handicapped people. As it is essential for people to go to bed at night (other medical problems can occur if a person sleeps in an armchair), solutions must be found.

Problem: The person is unable to get in and out of bed

The mattress may be very soft, making it difficult for the person to get a purchase on it in order to move himself on to and across the bed. A firm mattress will obviously be better but often the client is unable to afford to change his mattress. Bed boards placed underneath the mattress will help to firm it up. These are sometimes called fracture boards and are planks of wood placed across the width of the bed.

A "bed ladder" (Fig. 22) may also be needed to provide a handhold for the person to grip when moving himself on and off the bed. This is a ladder made of wooden or plastic dowels strung together with strong cord. It is attached to the bottom legs of the bed and comes over the covers and up to the middle of the bed. There are other aids which an occupational therapist may suggest and if the problems are extreme, she should be called in to give advice.

Fig. 22 Bed ladder

The bed may be too high to climb on, or too low, so that the person has to fall on to it. A low bed can be extremely difficult to rise from when getting out. If the bed is too high then the legs can be cut down providing that this is done by a technician, who will do it properly. If too low, then bed blocks can be used to raise it up to the required height. These are usually made of wood and the legs of the bed fit into them (Fig. 23). The best height of the bed is determined by finding a chair that the person uses which is the right height for him to get out of easily. The bed should be made the same height as this chair. The bed of a person permanently in a wheelchair needs to be of the same height as the wheelchair to facilitate an easy transfer sideways on to the bed.

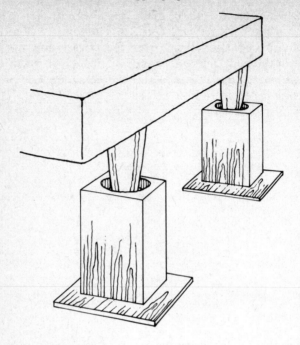

Fig. 23 Wooden bed blocks

Problem: *The person is unable to pull himself up in the bed*

A bed ladder can be useful for this movement and might be tried before other methods. Otherwise, an over-bed handle or "monkey pole" might help (Fig. 24). This is commonly used in hospital beds and fits to the bed frame behind the head of the bed. It extends across the person's head and at the end is a rope or chain with a handle which hangs down. The person, if he can reach up, can grip the handle and raise his bottom off the bed whilst digging his heels into the mattress. There are over-bed handles made which do not have to be attached to the bed, but are free-standing. These are useful with divan beds at home.

If the person is unable to get to his bedroom, particularly when it is up a flight of stairs which he is unable to manage, then there are two solutions open to him.

1. He can bring his bed downstairs and make a downstairs room into a bedroom.

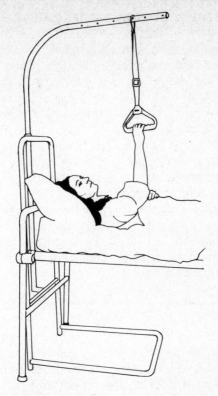

Fig. 24 Over-bed handle attached to the head of the bed

2. He can have a stairslift installed to carry him upstairs. This is very practical when he is an active person and needs to use the whole house, particularly when other facilities, such as the toilet and bathroom, are located upstairs. (Not all staircases are suitable for the installation of a stairslift. An occupational therapist should be asked for advice.)

Domestic activities

Preparing food

Cooking and preparing food are essential activities of daily life. If a person is to increase his independence, then he will need to be able to provide himself at least with breakfast and snacks during the day and at bedtime. A full dinner may

157

present considerable problems and the meals on wheels service may be necessary for the main hot meal of the day. However, there are often times when meals on wheels cannot be available and some kind of menu must be thought out.

Consideration should be given to a fairly balanced diet, with protein and fresh fruit and vegetables as well as the staple carbohydrates of bread and biscuits. *Kitchen Sense* (item 35 in the Bibliography at the end of this book), published by the Disabled Living Foundation, is an excellent book which goes into the activity of cooking and preparing food. It contains easily prepared recipes for one which are full of food value and yet easy on the purse.

An occupational therapist will be the person to help a physically handicapped client to relearn these activities when he is disabled. She will also consider adaptation and rearrangement of the kitchen with the client to ensure that everything can be within reach.

Housework

It is usually desirable for someone confined indoors through disability to be able to continue to look after the home. This is especially so with a disabled housewife, who may feel helpless and frustrated because she cannot do her housework as well as she used to. Even, or perhaps especially, when a home help is going into the home, the disabled woman will usually want to share the tasks. Many disabled women have said that a home help has given them a new interest in their home. She is another woman with whom to discuss the finer details, such as which curtains to put up, or how best to arrange a room. A home help may actively encourage a disabled woman to do some of the household tasks which are within her capabilities.

Again, an occupational therapist can often provide advice on structural changes or aids which will make these tasks easier to accomplish. For example, a duvet rather than traditional sheets and blankets will make bed making easier, curtain cords will facilitate the opening and closing of curtains and special window openers will facilitate this activity.

The resourceful home help will see many little tasks around the house that could be achieved independently and would help the disabled housewife to feel that she is not totally worthless and dependent.

16 Walking and wheelchair mobility

Importance of the pattern of walking

Walking is the name we casually give to one of the most complex activities which the human body ever learns to accomplish. We take it so much for granted that we do not pause to consider the complicated pattern of movements which makes up walking upright on two legs. What is more, once we have mastered walking in its simplest form we can then go on to refine it into running, jumping and dancing – and how much more complex it becomes! Let us look more closely at how walking develops.

An infant whilst still horizontal begins to straighten itself. First it pushes out its legs and extends its back; then, when it feels the pressure of something on the soles of its feet – maybe mother's hand – it thrusts against it in a stronger extension of its body. This is a purely reflex action which is stimulated by the sensation of pressure on the soles of the feet and is one of the first reflexes to be exercised in the development of upright standing. The baby rolls over on to its tummy, pushes down on its arms and lifts its head up, extending its back at the same time. When the neck and back muscles become stronger it is able to balance itself in a sitting position. Another reflex, the righting reflex, helps it to maintain this position without falling over sideways, forwards or backwards. Eventually it can even stretch out its arms, grasp something in its hand and bring that to its mouth without falling over. This practice exercises the sitting balance.

Now begins the exercise which strengthens the muscles of the pelvis and legs, crawling. Forwards or backwards, this is an important stage in increasing muscle power and joint mobility. When the time comes for standing, the baby will pull itself up with its arms on a piece of furniture or a person and, wobbling a little, will stand with feet apart to balance itself. It will give itself plenty of practice in standing, supporting itself, before it is able to let go, for then its balance will be put to the test. After many bumps down on its bottom from unsupported standing, it will begin to take its first steps and its parents will be suitably proud of its progress.

All of this movement is in response to an innate pattern of development which we have all experienced. It is dependent not only on the strengthening of muscles and the movement of joints but on a highly complex nervous system which has to develop its potential at the same time. For example, throughout all the movements described above, the brain is learning to interpret the position of all parts of the body in space so that movements can be adjusted to be effective and accurate.

If we now look at the normal healthy adult's pattern of walking we will see that he usually keeps his head upright, looking around with his eyes to check the ground in front of him and noticing any obstacles which he will circumnavigate, and he will plan his route. He will put one foot in front of the other, transferring his weight on to it and following through with the other foot. He will swing his arms as he walks, the opposite arm swinging forward with each step of the leg. In this rhythmical, flowing way he will be able to propel his body forwards whether it is rough or smooth ground, wet or dry, day or night. He will continue to breath rhythmically as he walks, the rate of breathing increasing as he uses more effort. All the muscles of the body are working in this activity but working with a rhythm which is relatively tireless.

Any illness which affects the brain, spinal cord, nerves, muscles, bones or joints will have an effect upon walking, as will diseases which give rise to inefficiency in blood circulation or breathing. Sometimes walking is seriously affected, in other conditions the effect is only slight.

When re-educating walking, the physiotherapist bears in mind the need to consider muscular and neurological patterns of activity, working from the basic development of walking. This will include practice in rolling and turning in bed, sitting and balancing, standing and balancing, feeling the ground beneath the feet and the position of the body in space, and then practice in taking steps, at first aided and then unaided. People who have suffered a stroke will have had their neurological control affected, sometimes severely, and will require considerable re-education, almost amounting to redevelopment of a walking pattern through all the stages.

People who have had legs amputated, either below knee or above knee, will need to learn to balance again without sensation in their artificial limbs.

Walking aids

The physiotherapist is mainly concerned with the exercise and re-education of walking after an illness and is the best person to advise on the use of walking aids. A spell in hospital or as an out-patient to the physiotherapy department will enable the correct walking aid to be selected and the person educated in its use.

A walking pattern has to be developed which will follow as closely as possible the normal rhythmic pattern so natural to the body. For example, watch a person who uses a walking stick to support him because his left knee is strained and painful and he cannot bear his full weight upon it. If he is using his stick correctly, he will hold it in his right hand. As he steps forward with his left leg he will place the stick forward as well, so that when he takes his weight on to the left leg he takes it also on to the stick; then he follows through with his right leg (Fig. 25). If the same man had two painful legs, he would use two sticks. Again the same pattern is used, opposite stick and leg moving together (Fig. 26).

A variety of different types of walking aids is prescribed for people depending upon their disability. Three points are important with all walking aids.

1. All walking aids rely on the arms supporting the body through the aid.
2. All walking aids should have non-slip ferrules on the end of the legs. In the case of wheels and castors, these should be checked from time to time to see that they are not "bald".
3. All walking aids should be correctly measured and adjusted to the right height for the individual. The correct height is determined by asking the person to stand up straight with his arms hanging loosely at his sides. Then

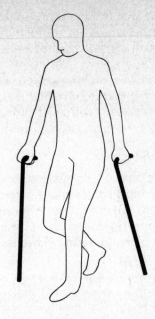

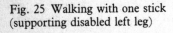

Fig. 25 Walking with one stick
(supporting disabled left leg)

Fig. 26 Walking with two sticks
(both legs disabled)

measure from his wrist to the ground and that will be
the height of the hand-hold of the aid. The measurement
of elbow and axilla supports is described below.

Types of walking aids

Some of the most common walking aids are illustrated in Fig.
27.

Axilla crutches

These are most frequently prescribed when a person is unable
or forbidden (in order to promote healing) to bear weight on
one leg. They enable a person to use the two crutches together
for step and the "good" leg for the other step. He need
not bear any weight on his affected leg and can just let it
swing. The hand-hold of the crutches is measured as described
above and then the axilla pad is adjusted to fit comfortably
into the armpit – *without pressure*.

162

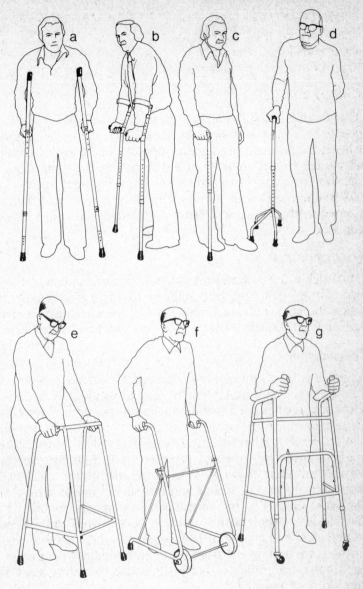

Fig. 27 Seven common types of walking aid: (a) axilla crutches (b) elbow crutches (c) walking stick (d) quadrapod stick (e) simple walking frame (f) walking frame with front wheels (g) frame with forearm gutters and front castors

Elbow crutches

These can be used in a similar way to axilla crutches; or, when both legs are weak, they can be used to support each step in turn, the opposite stick supporting the opposite leg.

Walking stick

The use of this aid has already been described. Many elderly people borrow a walking stick from a relative or neighbour when they begin to need some support. These sticks should always be checked to make sure that they are the right height. We have frequently met ladies who are using their husband's old walking cane and he was obviously a great deal taller! Consequently, the stick is just not providing the right kind of support.

Quadrapod stick

This stick is most often prescribed for those people who have had a stroke. The extra feet on the bottom give greater support when the stick is leaned upon. An added advantage is that the stick can be left to stand on its own without falling over.

Walking frame

This aid is most commonly prescribed for elderly people because it is so stable and gives a feeling of security to the user. However, it does not allow for the use of the normal walking pattern, with arms swinging, and therefore younger people (unless severely disabled) are not encouraged in its use. The frame is lifted forward and placed with all four feet on the ground and then, leaning on the frame, the person takes two steps forward into it. Frame and feet should not be moved at the same time. The use of this aid has brought mobility to many elderly people with stiff limbs, poor balance and general weakness. The hanging of handbags and other carrying bags on the arms and on the front of the frame should be discouraged unless carefully balanced, otherwise the safety asset of this aid is diminished.

Frame with front wheels

Sometimes elderly people have difficulty in lifting their frames forward, either because they are too heavy for weak arms or because the person cannot stand unsupported for long enough. Then this type of frame is useful because it can be pushed forwards. Weight can still be borne on it when walking into it, as it has back feet.

Frame with forearm gutters and front castors

This aid is rather large for use in a small house unless furniture is moved and doorways are wide. However, it is extremely useful for the person whose arms and hands are very weak, preventing him both from lifting the frame forwards and from bearing his weight on his extended arms. He rests his forearms in the gutters and leans on the aid to push it forward on the front castors. Then he steps into it. The height of the aid should be adjusted so that the gutters are level with the elbow when the person is standing upright.

When a person has a permanent walking difficulty and must rely on a walking aid, it often becomes an extension of his body, a part of him. Therefore, each person must have his own individual aid and should never have to share it with someone else. This is particularly important to remember in residential homes for the elderly or disabled. Also any change of type of walking aid should only be made in consultation with a remedial therapist, nurse or doctor, who will be aware of the reasons for changes in the person's mobility.

The use of artificial limbs

The majority of lower limb amputees are over the age of 65. Usually one or both legs have had to be amputated because of circulatory problems and ischaemia in the legs, which is chronic and untreatable in any other way. There has usually been intense pain and gangrene in the leg, bringing the surgeon to the conclusion that the leg should be amputated. In an ideal situation the person is prepared for the operation knowing that he will be rid of a painful limb which is impairing his walking. Ideally, again, preoperative exercise will be aimed at strengthening his arms and the other leg, and ensuring that his hips can be fully straightened for weight bearing. After the operation he will have a temporary leg (pylon) fitted which will have a "rocker" fitted to the bottom in place of a foot (Fig. 28). Walking on this will start within a week of the operation, as soon as the stump is sufficiently healed.

When both legs have been amputated above the knee two

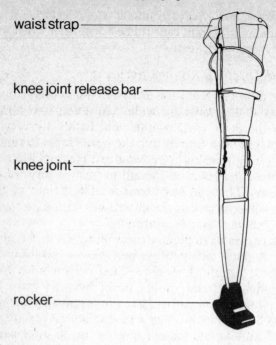

waist strap

knee joint release bar

knee joint

rocker

Fig. 28 Pylon with rocker foot, used in above-the-knee amputation

short pylons are fitted which are only about half the length of the legs. These make balancing a great deal easier.

Obviously getting used to walking without one's own legs is very difficult and normally crutches are used initially. Gradually the person will progress to a walking frame. He will eventually receive his permanent artificial limbs and cosmetic legs may be supplied for going out in a wheelchair.

A wheelchair is always prescribed for the elderly amputee. Even if he is able to walk indoors it is useful for going out; walking on rough ground is always more difficult with artificial legs. However, many above-knee amputees will require a wheelchair for use in the home as well. When both legs have been amputated the person's centre of gravity is altered when sitting: that is, he does not have the weight of his legs to balance him at the front. Therefore the wheelchair must have the back wheels set back to balance this, otherwise it will topple over backwards with the person in it. A harness may also be necessary to prevent the person from falling forwards out of the chair when he leans forward.

Wheelchair living

The international symbol of disability is a person in a wheelchair. When we think of "the disabled" the image of a wheelchair invariably springs to mind. In many ways this is hampering, because the majority of people with disabilities are not permanently sitting in wheelchairs and therefore designers of public buildings, houses, furniture, and so on need to appreciate this in order to design effectively for all disabled people, including those who are ambulant.

Because the wheelchair is the symbol of disability, when the suggestion is made that someone give up his walking for wheelchair living it has a profoundly serious significance. The person's self-image is challenged. How does he view himself? How disabled does he feel? Does he label himself as a "disabled" person?

There would seem to be two approaches to wheelchair living. One is the sudden approach; the paraplegic, following an accident, discovers that there is no use in his legs and is told that he will not be able to walk again. A wheelchair is the only way in which he will become mobile. He takes to a wheelchair first and examines its implications afterwards. To a certain extent he may be protected from the realisation of wheelchair dependence in a walking community by learning to use his wheelchair in a hospital environment where everything is geared to wheelchair living. It is when he returns home that he is forced to examine both the practical aspects of wheelchair living and the psychological aspects of his own and other people's attitudes.

The other approach to wheelchair living is the slow approach. The person's walking gradually deteriorates over a period of time, and pain and stiffness, loss of balance and frequent falls may cause him frustration. He may be examining his image of disability in himself and may either accept the use of a wheelchair as a positive step or reject it because it will confirm the fact that he is a disabled person. If he has accepted a wheelchair for "going out in the car" of "for holidays", he will have begun to experience the advantages (and disadvantages) already. Many people, however, "would not be seen dead in a wheelchair" outside their homes.

When a person's mobility becomes severely affected it is usually time that he was reassessed medically by a specialist doctor. The referral to the specialist is made by the patient's family practitioner. The medical assessment will usually take place at an out-patient clinic or day hospital where the doctor will also call upon the physiotherapist and the occupational therapist to assess the patient's function. There will be discussion with the patient about his mobility problems and possible solutions. The question of a wheelchair is best raised at this point when the patient is able, with help, to examine his feelings about his disability. The hospital social worker will often be involved in helping him to see the reality of his situation.

The decision to prescribe a wheelchair is made by the doctor – GP or specialist – in consultation with nurses and therapists when, and only when, it is felt that the advantages of a wheelchair existence far outweigh the disadvantages.

Reasons for wheelchair living include the following:

1. The person is totally unable to be sufficiently mobile at home to continue to live a normal daily life on his feet.
2. He is able to perform his daily living activities only with great pain and so slowly that his routine is severely affected; for instance, he is unable to choose and enjoy any stimulating activity because his time is completely taken up with the basic essentials of moving about, toileting, etc.
3. His health is severely affected by the effort of walking.

One reason against wheelchair living is that if a person is prevented from walking by the premature prescription of a wheelchair, his health will suffer in that he will quickly lose function by becoming stiff and weak and losing the motivation to move.

As can be seen, there is often a very fine boundary between the desirability of wheelchair independence and the retaining of ambulant independence. Then the decision can be a particularly difficult one. *It is important, however, that a decision is actually taken.* In some institutional settings where spare wheelchairs are available for emergencies, a person may prematurely gravitate to wheelchair use because this is most convenient for the institution's staff. One example is where a person is incontinent because he can walk the distance to the toilet but takes some time, with consequent "accidents". It is convenient to push him to the toilet quickly in a wheelchair and once he is back in the sitting room, it is convenient to let him continue to sit in the wheelchair ready for the next time he wants to go to the toilet. It is then a very short time before that person becomes wheelchair-bound, stiff and weak through lack of exercise and unable to walk. If the decision is made that he should stay in the wheelchair as a better alternative to walking, then he must be taught how to use the wheelchair independently, to propel himself, toilet himself and transfer from the chair to an armchair, toilet or bed. However, I have seen such a person who was quicker getting around on his legs than he was in the wheelchair because he had extreme difficulty in propelling it around. The problem in that instance just had not been thought out before a decision was reached.

The right wheelchair

Wheelchairs, such as those in Fig. 29, are supplied free of charge by the Department of Health and Social Security from one of their regional Artificial Limb and Appliance Centres (ALAC). Family practitioners and hospital doctors and specialists are able to prescribe a wheelchair by sending the appropriate form to the ALAC in their region. The choice of chair is stated on the form and there are a number of optional extras which can be selected at this time, such as seat cushions, detachable trays and elevating leg rests.

The choice of the right chair for the individual will depend upon his ability to propel the chair and transfer from the chair, and upon the dimensions of both himself and his home (width of doorways and passages). It is desirable in most instances, where the chair will be in constant use, that the person is given the opportunity to try out several models before one is ordered, for the selection of the right chair is vital to the person's adjustment to wheelchair living. Many hospitals have a regular wheelchair clinic where a variety of models can be seen and tried. These clinics are often attended by a technical officer from the ALAC, together with a doctor who will assess the person medically and make the necessary prescription.

Children and young adults are almost always assessed in this way but elderly people often do not get the chance of this

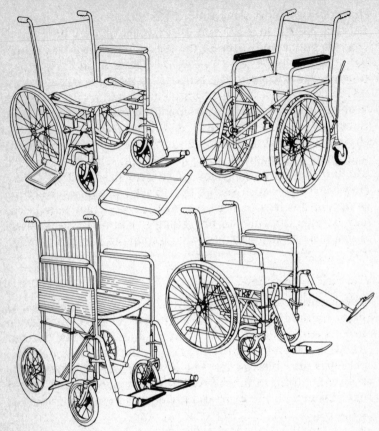

Fig. 29 Four of the many models of wheelchair available

service, as forms are sent directly from the GP to the ALAC and the first time the person sees his wheelchair is when it is delivered to his home. Social services staff might suggest to the GP that a visit to the local wheelchair clinic may be beneficial for the person before a wheelchair is ordered, to make sure that he knows beforehand what he is getting.

Technical officers will do home visits where a person is not finding his chair entirely suitable and where there are individual problems due to deterioration in his function. Occupational therapists working in the community will often visit with the technical officer so that the most appropriate chair can be selected and adaptations to the home can be considered where necessary.

In addition to the manual self-propelled wheelchairs described above there is an indoor, electrically propelled model available for a person who cannot use his arms to propel a chair. There is also an attendant-controlled electric outdoor chair to enable a relative or friend to take the person out when he is too heavy for them to push in an ordinary chair. This is especially useful to an elderly couple, where the partner may find it difficult to push an ordinary chair because of his or her own frailty. Both of these chairs are ordered in the same way as previously described but the person and relative are asked to attend the ALAC for practice in the use of the powered chair. Enquiries are also made by the DHSS as to whether there is undercover storage space for the outdoor chair and the facility to recharge the batteries.

The great gap in provision is for *self-operated* electric outdoor wheelchairs. Many of these chairs are available on the market and are much more expensive to buy than manual chairs. Unfortunately, neither the DHSS nor local authority social services departments provide them. It is left to the person himself, or a voluntary society on his behalf, to raise the money to buy the chair privately. These chairs are usually driven on the pavement and are capable of travelling only short distances at a brisk walking pace. However, they are very useful for local shopping and visiting neighbouring houses. Some second-hand models are available from time to time and are usually advertised in the journals of national and local societies for the disabled. If a person is contemplating the purchase of this type of chair he would be well advised to try out several models before he makes his choice, to ensure that he is able to control the chair. Many firms will give a demonstration in the person's own home and the Disabled Living Foundation's permanent exhibition shows several models which can be tried out.

Learning to use a wheelchair

Propelling the chair

The large propelling wheels of the wheelchair are usually placed at the back of the chair (small castors at the front) to enable the person to adopt a comfortable posture, with the

171

back supported by the backrest and the head up. The person's arms should then fall naturally on to the outer propelling rims of the back wheels. When moving straight ahead both rims are gripped as far back as possible and pushed forward together as far as the reach will take them. The hands are then slid back together round the rims and again pushed forwards. It is important, especially for long distances out of doors, for a rhythm to be developed to prevent tiring.

When turning the chair, either one wheel is held still – on the side to be turned towards – and the other wheel is pushed forwards, or for a more brisk turn one wheel is pushed forwards while the other is pulled back. A very sharp turn can be made by this method.

A wheelchair can be selected which has the large propelling wheels at the front, for the person whose shoulders prevent him from reaching back with his arms or who cannot sit up straight. This is not, however, a good posture for normal use.

Negotiating passages, doorways and furniture indoors comes with practice but some alteration may be needed to the arrangement of furniture. Carpets which are very thick and are not fitted wall-to-wall and rugs can be difficult to negotiate without considerable effort, and thought should be given to abandoning the use of mats. Doorways may need to be made wider, doors hung round the other way or sliding doors fitted. Creation of space becomes all-important for the wheelchair user. In the event of insoluble structural problems being encountered, the person may consider rehousing into more suitable accommodation.

Transferring

Transferring from the wheelchair is required for getting on to the toilet and into the bath, getting in and out of bed and sitting in any alternative chair. It is accomplished in whichever way is easiest for the individual and can be either forward or sideways transfer.

Forward transfer usually relies upon the person being able to support himself on his legs for long enough to be able to swing through 180 degrees. It is a useful method of transfer when there is limited space, as in small toilets. Rails are usually required either at the sides of the toilet or on the wall behind the toilet pan (this is not possible with a low-level cistern).

Sideways transfer does not rely on the weight being borne on the legs. The arm of the wheelchair is removed, the chair brought alongside the seat and the bottom lifted or slid across, using the arms to bear the weight. Sometimes a piece of wood or transfer board is handy to bridge the gap between seats and the bottom is slid along this board. It is essential, for easy transfer, to have both seats (the wheelchair seat and the seat to which the transfer is to be made) the same height. The only possible way to raise the height of the wheelchair seat is with cushions (a plywood base to the cushion will give it additional firmness). It is often easier to raise the height of the other seat – a toilet by a raised toilet seat; a bed by the use of bed blocks and a chair by the use of blocks under the legs.

The most important point that the person must train himself to remember when transferring is *always* to put the wheelchair brakes on *before* he transfers. The footrests must also be raised, removed or swung out of the way.

The severely handicapped person may be able to use an electric hoist independently for transferring. This will be particularly appropriate for the bath, which involves complex movements in getting in and out. An Autolift bath hoist (see p. 152) may help the person who can transfer on to its seat. An electric overhead track hoist (Fig. 30) may be useful, as it can be operated by pull cord controls to take the person up, across and down into the bath. A sling is used under the person for attachment to this type of hoist. The same hoist is also useful to enable the person to get in and out of bed independently, or from the bed on to a commode.

Getting in and out of a car

The use of a car is absolutely essential for the independent disabled person. The Motability scheme enables people to lease a car using their mobility allowance in payment (see p. 223). Transferring into a car seat can be accomplished independently in one of three ways.

1. The wheelchair is brought alongside the open car door, the brakes are applied and the side of the wheelchair is removed. Then the bottom is lifted across on to the car seat using the power in the arms, either before or after the legs have been lifted in.

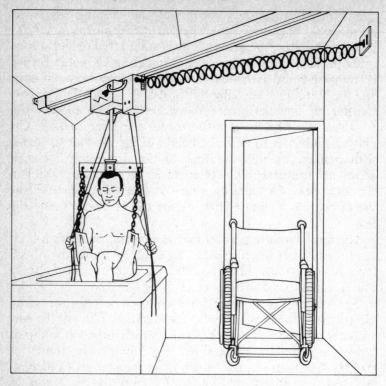

Fig. 30 Electric overhead track hoist

2. If the person can bear weight on his legs, he may bring
   the wheelchair alongside the open car door, apply the
   brakes and remove the armrest, then pull himself up,
   using the car frame, and swing round, lowering his
   bottom on to the seat. He pulls his legs in after him.
3. A sliding-swivelling car seat adaptor (for bucket-type car
   seats only) can be purchased; it fits under the car seat
   and enables it to be pulled sideways out of the car and
   then swivelled round for easy transfer. After the transfer
   is made the seat is swivelled back to face the front and
   slid back into the car, the legs are lifted in on the way.

There is a car-top hoist which can be used by another person
to transfer the handicapped person into the car seat. This
hoist remains permanently fitted to the roof of the car. How-

ever, before purchase a check should be made with the manufacturers of the hoist, as it does not fit every make of car.

The main problem in independent motoring is that most people have difficulty in lifting their wheelchair into the car after themselves. This problem can sometimes be overcome by careful thought and manoeuvring but many people have to seek help when they would otherwise be independent. One solution to this problem is to keep two wheelchairs, one for inside the car (when help will still be needed at the destination), and one at home, strategically placed in the car port or garage. This will enable the person at least to get back home independently. Adaptations to cars are very difficult, although some work is being done on alternative designs of cars for disabled drivers.

Access

Access is one of the most burning issues of our time where the physically handicapped are concerned. To enable a physically handicapped person to participate fully in the world in which he lives that world must be physically accessible to him. Places of work, entertainment and sport, shops, restaurants, banks and all public services should be housed in accessible buildings to which and within which there is access either for the person in a wheelchair or the ambulant disabled person.

In 1977 the Silver Jubilee Committee on Access for the Disabled was established to work on the promotion of this ideal throughout Britain. A report of that work was published by the DHSS, entitled *Can Disabled People Go Where You Go?* There is much comment in the report on badly planned new buildings which restrict the access of disabled people because of the lack of accessible lavatories, steps up to the entrance, high kerbs with few dropped areas, shops with turnstiles, no adjacent parking spaces and so on. It is acknowledged that old buildings may be difficult to adapt but there are often ways round the problem, given the right attitudes, understanding and goodwill. There is little excuse for the architect of a new building who does not make provision for disabled people.

The biggest stumbling blocks in the access campaign are the Fire Regulations Act 1971 and the Health and Safety at Work Act 1974. Both of these acts impose considerable restrictions in building design that prevent free access for disabled people in general and wheelchair users in particular. There is a danger that, in the pursuit of safety, a significant proportion of the general public will be barred from using buildings altogether.

Attitudes to access need changing, by law if necessary, and disabled people themselves need to be given the opportunity to contribute to planning and policy. The establishment of local voluntary access groups and the publishing of local access guides is recommended. It is also recommended in the report that local authority planning departments should issue guidance on the requirements of the Chronically Sick and Disabled Persons Act (see Chapter 8) to everyone intending to put up a public building or facility.

Following the Silver Jubilee Committee's report, a new committee has been formed – the Committee on Restrictions Against the Disabled (CORAD). This Committee will continue to publicise disabled people's needs, "monitor developments arising out of the Health and Safety at Work Act and the Fire Precautions Act and give advice before any regulations or new laws are introduced about what impact they could have on disabled people." It is hoped that this campaign will be successful and that access will be improved for the benefit of all disabled people. Such improvements will also benefit the able-bodied, who often have prams to push and heavy loads to carry.

17 Management of incontinence

Incontinence is a word used to describe the condition when control of the bladder or bowel is weakened or lost. Loss of bladder control is described as urinary incontinence and loss of bowel control is called faecal incontinence. Both have considerable social consequences for a person and incontinence itself is extremely disabling both physically and psychologically. Fortunately faecal incontinence is less common than incontinence of urine and so it is on urinary incontinence that this chapter mainly concentrates.

Urinary incontinence can be caused by temporary illness, after childbirth, by infections of the bladder or womb and by disease or injury to the nervous system. It is very common after a stroke, though it may not be lasting. The decreased mobility of elderly people may be responsible for accidents when the person is not able to get to a lavatory quickly enough. When a person starts to become incontinent, he should always be referred to a doctor for investigation to see whether the cause can be treated.

There are various kinds of urinary incontinence.

1. There may be a need to pass water much more often, both during the day and during the night. This is described as frequency.
2. There may be very little warning of the need to empty the bladder. The person gets the warning and then must go very quickly afterwards; he cannot hold himself. This is described as urgency.
3. There may be a leaking of urine most of the time with very little awareness of the person that he wants to pass water. This is dribbling incontinence.

4. In women there may be a slight leakage when coughing, laughing or sneezing. This is called stress incontinence.

If the incontinence is due to a treatable cause such as infection, then the doctor will prescribe medication to cure it. A temporary catheter may be used after a stroke or spinal injury until the person can be re-educated to empty his bladder at appropriate times. A catheter is a flexible tube inserted into the bladder which enables urine to be drained into a bag. Stress incontinence in younger people can be treated by teaching exercises designed to strengthen the muscles of the pelvic floor.

Methods of combating incontinence

1. A commode can be kept conveniently near to the elderly person so that he does not have to walk a long way to his toilet. Commodes are usually supplied by local community health departments.
2. People confined to bed or to a chair may need a portable urinal close by which they can use regularly. These are available in designs for both men and women and local health departments supply them. A special mattress and cushion are also available (Easinurse) which hold a receptacle underneath. For more details see p. 125.
3. If the bladder can be routinely emptied in the normal way every two hours this can reduce incontinence. Once the person gets into a regular pattern this will become easy to remember but, to begin with, an ordinary kitchen timer might be used to remind him.
4. If there is a problem in getting to the toilet, or managing once there, then aids and adaptations might be useful (see Chapter 15). Clothing can also be chosen for easier management.
5. Many people cut down on their fluid intake hoping that this will prevent incontinence. This is a great mistake and can lead to other medical problems. It is better to drink normally in the early part of the day while still mobile, and to reduce the fluid intake later, having the last drink a few hours before bedtime.
6. It is important to try to move the bowels regularly. Constipation can aggravate urinary incontinence. A diet which includes fresh fruit and vegetables and plenty of

liquids will help to regulate the bowels. Many elderly people have their own dietary remedies for constipation and do not need laxatives. It is important that laxatives are only taken on the advice of a doctor or nurse as they can often be damaging to health if taken indiscriminately.

Aids and appliances

A large variety of different types of pads and pants is available and can usually be obtained through the local community health department; supplies are usually delivered regularly. Each authority tends to keep its own particular preferred selection. Underpads are also available from the same source for use on beds and chairs, as is plastic sheeting, which goes under the bottom sheet and protects the mattress. A special type of bed sheet is now being marketed which incorporates an absorbent lining so that the surface remains dry. This is considered to be extremely effective because it avoids the skin remaining in contact with a wet surface during the night.

People with nervous disorders which cause loss of sensation and consequent lack of awareness of the need to pass water may have an appliance fitted which will collect the urine. This may incorporate a catheter or some kind of sheath or funnel, and a bag. These appliances are individually chosen and fitted on prescription from a doctor. Some hospitals provide a skilled fitting service from firms of surgical suppliers.

Incontinence laundry service

Most authorities provide a collection, laundry and delivery service for sheets in cases where there is a considerable amount of washing because of incontinence. Local health departments also make a regular collection of soiled pads for disposal.

Artificial openings (stomata)

Although they do not strictly come under the heading of incontinence, a mention should be made of the management of artificial openings which have been surgically produced by colostomy and ileostomy in the treatment of chronic diseases of the bowels. The bowel is opened on to the surface of the abdomen (the hole is called a stoma) and the faeces are collected by means of a bag worn close to the body. After the operation, the person is fitted with the appropriate appliance and taught how to use it and how and when to change it. He is also taught about a diet which will facilitate the passing of motions, and foodstuffs which are to be avoided because they produce excessive wind or odour.

People who have physical disabilities which make changing the bags difficult will require help to remain independent in managing their stomata. Advice should be sought from the community nurse for these people. These operations can have serious psychological effects upon the recipients and it is worth contacting the Colostomy Welfare Group or the Ileostomy Association of Great Britain and Northern Ireland (see Chapter 11), who have welfare workers, themselves having gone through the operation, to counsel and advise people.

The disposal of soiled bags may be found to be a problem. Most people rinse them out in the toilet, wrap them in plenty of newspaper and put them in the dustbin but an elderly disabled person may find this difficult. The collection service for soiled pads may then be needed.

Control of odour

Often the most worrying aspect of incontinence is smell. People are worried that their affliction will be obvious to others and that they will be further isolated because people will find them unpleasant to be near. A few elderly people, whose sense of smell is dulled by the fact that they have grown accustomed to the odour of incontinence, may find that people do not visit so often or move away from them when they are in a social group.

In each situation, it is important to be aware of the sensitive nature of the subject, whilst tactfully advancing help and advice to the person so that he may take steps to control the smell of incontinence, both on his person and in his home.

Personal freshness can be maintained by regular washing, both of the person and of his clothes. The application of commercial deodorants can never take the place of soap and water. Underclothes, incontinence garments and pads, etc., should be changed frequently and it is necessary to ensure that the person has adequate supplies to hand. Top clothes can be protected by the use of plastic pants and easily laundered fabrics should be chosen for dresses, trousers, etc., when there is an incontinence problem.

Special incontinence appliances (body worn) should be

regularly and thoroughly cleaned, preferably daily, and it is therefore necessary to have two appliances, one off and one on. An antiseptic such as Dettol or Savlon, which will not affect the rubber parts, should be used in warm water and it is also important to make sure that they are quite dry before putting on.

Smell in the house can be prevented by regular and thorough ventilation of rooms, especially the bedroom, toilet and bathroom. Bed linen should be changed frequently and plastic sheeting used to protect the mattress under the bottom sheet. Plastic covers can also be used on armchairs, under a washable fitted cover. It is most often the impregnation of furniture and carpets with urine which accounts for permanent smell in the house. The application of a neutralising deodorant like Nilodor to water used for washing commodes, floors and carpets will help and this can also be used for urinals and bedpans which are in use.

Soiled disposables should be wrapped up immediately and stored in a lidded receptacle until thrown away or collected. Soiled linen should be rinsed out and put into soak with Napisan as quickly as possible. Modern automatic washing machines and tumble dryers are absolutely invaluable for the household with an incontinent member and it is worth while for the social services worker to consider ways of obtaining these essential aids which, alas, are not supplied by social services departments. Some charities are willing to help with the cost, especially the Family Fund (address on p. 106), which exists to help families with severely handicapped children. Charities which help disabled adults can also be found and second-hand, reconditioned washing machines are available to reduce the cost.

The above is necessarily a very brief description of the management of incontinence. Readers are referred to the excellent literature and advice available from the Incontinence Advisory Service of the Disabled Living Foundation (address on p. 106). The DLF publish two leaflets: *Urinary Incontinence – Guidelines for Professional Staff* and *Notes on Incontinence*, which is produced for incontinence sufferers. This organisation will answer any queries which disabled people or professional staff have about the problems of incontinence and the range of equipment which is available.

18 Sexual problems and disability

We live at a time when the inheritance of over a century of sexual hypocrisy and repression has made its mark upon society. We are now said to be in an age of sexual permissiveness, which would seem to be a reaction against the age which has gone before. However, it is more an age of obsession with sexual matters rather than true permissiveness; for although permission exists on the one hand, on the other there is still a strong body of objection to free sexual expression, whether it be heterosexual or homosexual. In recent years attitudes to handicapped people have also changed, so that the "general public's" eyes are opened to the fact that people with disabilities are the same as anyone else, with the same needs and desires and the same rights to live a free and full life. However, attitudes run deep and, while many of us are wrestling with feelings about sexuality and are measuring ourselves against the various norms which are being advocated, feelings about the personality of disabled people being equal to our own are often harder to accept in relation to their sexuality. In theory we appreciate the importance to everyone of deep personal relationships and would not deny that anyone, with whatever disability, shares the same needs. In practice, however, we are unlikely to be willing to allow the handicapped teenager to experiment sexually as other teenagers do, or the resident of a home to sleep with another resident.

SPOD, the Committee for Sexual and Personal Relationships of the Disabled, has been instrumental in highlighting the whole subject of sexuality and disability and is making disabled people and professionals aware of the need for understanding, education and action in this area of human need. Interest and understanding is engendered through the emergence of many important publications on this subject (some listed in the Bibliography, p. 248). Education and action is being promoted through the work of SPOD in running seminars and training courses in counselling and in sex education for a variety of people whose work brings them into contact with the personal problems of disabled people. Organisations such as the Family Planning Association, the Marriage Guidance Council, the Multiple Sclerosis Society of Great Britain and the Spinal Injuries Association have also recognised the need for work in this area.

The majority of social services workers will, at some time, encounter disabled clients with problems in their sexual and personal relationships. As we have seen throughout the preceding chapters, disability can change abilities and social roles and the social worker is concerned with the person's adjustment in *all* respects. Undue emphasis should not be placed on sexual activity, lest its importance become magnified in an otherwise satisfactory situation. However, there should always be an awareness of the sexual component of relationships, in which the person may have considerable problems that he may need help to overcome.

Problems of the congenitally disabled

Many of those people who are born with cerebral palsy or spina bifida have motor and spatial problems which may lead to an unreal or distorted body image. There has usually been a considerable amount of handling of these young people throughout their lives by nurses, and therapists who have been concerned with movement and bodily functions but usually with an asexual approach. Little accent has been placed upon sexual function and in the special schools there is often a lack of sex education related to the individual child's understanding of his or her own body. However, in television and other media there is a great emphasis placed upon sexuality and on people's expectations of sexual experience. This often leads to confusion in the young person as to what it is all about and a naivety in the relationships which he forms. Added to this, because of his physical disabilities there is also a limitation of his own physical experiences with others. He does not have the experience of childish horseplay leading to touching, stroking and exploring of his body and those of his friends. He may not have been taught or be able to masturbate, so that he does not understand about sexual arousal and orgasm.

Parents who may have been unable to allow their child to mature at a normal pace need help to realise that he is growing up and at 18 years of age will be in control of his own future. As with parents of able-bodied children, there is a fine balance between protection of the child against hurt and exploitation and encouragement of him towards psychological and social independence. All parents have to adjust to the emerging sexuality of their children.

The Spastics Society runs occasional three-day counselling courses for spastic couples who want to get married. Usually three or four couples attend together and discuss the practical aspects of marriage, accommodation, finance, personally caring for each other, dressing, feeding, toileting and so on, and exploring their feelings for each other. These courses are carefully handled, for couples are often testing out their freedom for the first time and problems may arise if they are going to live together in a residential home, as will be seen later.

In local communities congenitally disabled young people may attend day centres for work and recreation and the relationships which are formed there can provide a basis for maturation, providing that staff are trained to use the day centre situation to advantage. The day centre could be an ideal place for group work and individual counselling of young people in sexual relationships and in social independence, for often it is the only place where the young adult is away from his parents and is able to assert his individuality. Such counselling would become part of a general programme towards social independence, including shopping and budgeting, travel and recreational prospects in the local community and aspects of social behaviour and friendships. Sex education might also be included for those who had missed out on this subject at school.

Problems of disabled adults

As we have seen in preceding chapters, long-term illness and disability may strain personal relationships in many ways, including sexually. These stresses occur because of:

1. Changes in role, including the masculine or feminine

role of the person, and loss of self-image and self-confidence.

2. Changes in sexual performance caused by loss of mobility, loss of or reduced sexual drive and physical and psychological problems of arousal.

3. Anxiety and depression may have an effect upon sexual interest and performance and the self-preoccupation which illness often brings will affect the way a person treats his or her partner.

4. There may be an accentuation of previous relationship difficulties due to impairment of sexual performance and interest. It is not uncommon for a man or woman who has always had a low sexual drive to use their illness as an excuse to halt sexual relations altogether.

5. Expectations may need to be changed; for example, with inability to conceive or danger of conception and childbirth (either for mother or baby).

The social worker, in considering the way in which illness or handicap has affected existing relationships, will include the sexual component of the relationship in her reckoning. The social worker in the hospital setting is especially aware and is able to help the person (or couple) to express sexual fears or difficulties at an early stage of adjustment and many hospital social workers have become very experienced in sexual counselling. Occupational therapists, physiotherapists and speech therapists, because of their particular role in treatment, also have found the need for education and training in sexual counselling.

Sexual problems in residential homes

Many of the problems in residential institutions are caused by the institution and its staff taking over the role of parents and custodians and becoming over-protective of residents. The making and breaking of relationships, which normally can cause hurt to individuals but nevertheless is an essential part of life experience and maturation, is guarded against by staff who feel that they must cushion residents against upset.

Often there is a lack of social opportunity and choice in the fixed community of the home, especially where there is little contact with the wider community outside. The person who is unable to find a compatible partner, especially the homosexual person, is trapped in this type of community.

Multibedded rooms provide no privacy for intimate meetings and even in single rooms the staff tend to open doors without knocking or knock on the door when it is locked. (A spastic couple who married while in a residential home pressed to leave because they were very often interrupted when they were making love.) The attitude of the management of homes will be cautious about sexual activity which might cause a scandal, even though the sexual expression may be normal and legitimate.

The attitudes of staff are gradually changing, with improved training courses available. The Cheshire Foundation runs its own training schemes for the staff of the Cheshire Homes and these schemes stress the importance of sexual and personal relationships and help staff to examine their attitudes.

The availability of counselling for residents is an important consideration and there are differing views as to whether this should be provided by special counsellors who come into the home or whether it can be done by the residential staff themselves. The arguments for and against each view are set out in *Counselling in a Residential Setting* (item 53 in the Bibliography at the end of this book). The Cheshire Foundation also provide counsellors who go into the homes on a regular basis as it is felt that skilled counselling is required because of the special problems which residential care imposes.

A different issue, the subject of much discussion at the moment, is whether or not residential staff should aid residents in sexual activity. Because of the high level of help with personal activities which severely disabled residents require, it has been suggested that staff should be able to help by lifting them into position for sexual intercourse and also aid with masturbation for the relief of sexual tension. It is a difficult issue, for it implies the possible psychological involvement of the helper and the need for deep concern and understanding, as well as a certain detachment. The depth of relationship of staff with residents is also a question raised in this context.

Some people have suggested that disabled people are entitled to help as they have the same right to sexual satisfaction as anyone else. Others have argued against this view on a variety of grounds. It has been found that complications arise when residential staff become emotionally involved with those in their care. Most professional staff have a code of conduct which prohibits sexual involvement with clients as the ensuing jealousies, tensions and frustrations could destroy the helping relationship. Most people, disabled or otherwise, feel very strongly that the expression of sexual feelings and indeed affection is a very private act and they would rather not have intercourse at all than have it in the presence of a third person, even if they are able to perform in these circumstances. Both viewpoints are worth consideration, as they arise from a genuine concern for the rights of disabled people.

Informing, advising and counselling

In enabling clients to talk about sexual difficulties, it is important to be able to use the client's own phraseology and language so that an understanding can develop about what is actually being expressed. It is also important to know the nature and possible prognosis of the disease, so that advice is practical and related to the real situation, and it is necessary to use direct questions about sex, for the more caution the social worker uses, so the more cautiously the client approaches the subject. Where people have sexual difficulties they will usually be glad of the opportunity to discuss these with someone.

Having enabled the disabled client to express his sexual problems, the social worker will then need to decide whether he needs information only or advice and/or expert counselling. It should not be taken for granted that everyone needs counselling, for the sexual problems of many disabled people are purely practical and given the right information such people are quite capable of trying out different techniques without discussing their feelings and relationships with a social worker.

Information and advice will be based on a knowledge of diseases and the sexual and physical limitations which they impose, and a knowledge of practical ways in which these limitations can be overcome in whole or in part. The reader is referred to the Bibliography to this book. Many books on specific diseases include a section on sexual problems. Of particular interest, *Not Made of Stone* by K. Heslinga and *The Sexual Side of Handicap* by W. F. R. Stewart are recommended because they include a wealth of information about disabling diseases and practical solutions to sexual problems. SPOD, already mentioned on p. 112, produces booklets which are useful for disabled people to read and many of the voluntary societies representing different diseases produce their own booklets of sexual information.

Counselling is best undertaken by a skilled counsellor and the client can be referred to SPOD at Brook House, 2–16 Torrington Place, London WC1 (telephone 01–637 4712), who will put him or her in touch with one of their own sexual counsellors, who are available all over the country. Social workers who are interested in counselling may wish to attend one of the regular SPOD counselling courses.

It should be remembered that sexual counselling is rather different to marital counselling, although the latter may include the former. If couples have severe marital problems they should be encouraged to seek marriage guidance. Marriage guidance counsellors are becoming increasingly aware of the various problems inherent in physical handicap. The Marriage Guidance Council runs local counselling services and addresses can be obtained from the central office at 76a New Cavendish Street, London W1. The Catholic Marriage Advisory Service provides sexual counselling, marriage guidance and advice on family planning and conception to Catholic couples. There are over 60 centres all over the country and the address for local help can be obtained from the central office at 15 Lansdowne Road, London W11 (telephone 01–727 0141).

Particular problems and practical solutions

It should be remembered that there are many inhibitions attached to methods of sexual expression and it may be difficult for couples to try alternative ways because these are thought of as "kinky", dirty or even depraved. The disabled person and his or her partner may require "permission" to be given by the counsellor ("you can do it this way, it is alright") before he can change. Even then there may be some methods which they cannot bring themselves to try. Here are some of the physical problems encountered, together with possible solutions which might be suggested.

Problem	*Solution*
1. Favourite positions are no longer possible or comfortable. (e.g. pain can cause physical and/or psychological barriers to sex. This can happen with rheumatoid arthritis, osteoarthrosis, stroke, multiple sclerosis, back injuries, etc.)	Try different positions, e.g. man lying supine, or woman lying on her side allowing rear entry Try use of aids, pillows, foam, to support the legs, back, etc. A vibrator can be a good substitute for hands when hands do not function Try oral sex or mutual masturbation if coitus impossible Try pain-relieving or anxiety-relieving drugs – on a doctor's advice. However, some drugs depress sexual urges and sensation
2. Loss of sensation around genital area. This can happen in spinal injury and spina bifida	Try using erogenous zones above the level of the lesion and exploring alternative areas of sensory stimulation by hands, mouth, vibrator, etc.
3. Impotence – erection not possible. Erection can be either reflex or psychogenic. Reflex means that it happens in response to direct tactile stimulation of the genitals. Psychogenic means erection in response to psychological stimulation such as sight, sound or sexual fantasy. Complete impotence occurs in high, complete spinal lesions accompanied by flaccid paralysis of limbs	Try "stuffing": the woman stuffs the flaccid penis into her vagina and moves herself upon it. For the man there is the possibility of psychological orgasm Try the use of an artificial penis strapped over the real one. This can give satisfaction to the female partner and hence the man. Psychological orgasm may be possible

189

4. Erection cannot be sustained. This can happen with spinal injuries resulting in spastic paralysis. Reflex erection needs constant stimulation to sustain. With spina bifida, reflex and psychogenic erections are possible in some cases

Try use of penile ring which helps to sustain erection

Try positions which will give more constant penis stimulation, e.g. man supine, woman on top

Try mutual stimulation by hand, mouth or vibrator

5. Premature ejaculation, and spasm of muscles. These problems occur together in cerebral palsy because of heightened reflexes

The doctor may prescribe valium to be taken before sexual intercourse. This has the effect of reducing spasm and may delay ejaculation

6. Incontinence appliance, (usually catheter) gets in the way. This can happen in any disease where this is used

Tape tube to tummy with adhesive tape so that it is out of the way. Make sure bags are empty if worn

7. Colostomy or ileostomy bag gets in the way

Make sure bag is empty and body is clean. Tape bag securely in place to the body

Try rear entry positions if woman wears a bag

If man wears a bag try positions where bodies are not in total contact. For different positions see *The Joy of Sex* by Alex Comfort

8. Need to urinate during coitus. This can sometimes occur at orgasm in people with stroke or spinal injuries

Make sure bladder is emptied just before intercourse. If it does happen, urine is sterile, make sure partner is cleaned up

9. Defaecation can sometimes happen during coitus due to reflex emptying of the bowel

It is best, where possible, to make love after the bowels have been emptied particularly where this has been found to be a problem

Dr Robert Chartham's *Sex Manners for Men* and *Mainly for Women* are useful books to recommend to clients. A variety of sexual methods and positions are described in a light and sympathetic way.

The matter of personal hygiene should be encouraged, not only where there are problems of incontinence but because sexual interest is sustained by clean, soft skin, and perfumes for men and women can aid sexual arousal.

The social services worker will want to sound out the level of acceptance of the individual person or couple to alternative methods and encourage an ability and willingness to experiment to find the best way of making love, teaching each other and letting each other know what is pleasing.

19 Housing needs

The idea is somehow ingrained in people's minds that the only suitable housing for a physically handicapped person is that designed to special wheelchair standards and dimensions, i.e. the specially designed disabled person's bungalow. There are, as we have seen, a wide variety of handicapping conditions which fortunately do not need resort to wheelchair living. Families come in various sizes and are often interested in normal houses of all ages (those with age and character being preferable to many who would not want to live in a new dwelling). Given the fact that a person may be living in a house of which he is extremely fond, in an area which completely suits his way of life, it seems rash to imagine that if he becomes disabled he will want to move out into a different house in a new area.

There are, however, those people who are entirely wheelchair bound and, in order to be independent, do require the extra space and design features which can be achieved only in a specially built dwelling. For those people, plus those with deteriorating conditions, it has been estimated that the specially designed provision needed is 1.6 dwellings per 1,000 population.

Most local authorities give consideration to two factors; what dwellings can be newly built with special features incorporated from the beginning, and what existing dwellings can be adapted to make them suitable to accommodate disabled people. For those people living in privately owned accommodation the Housing Act 1974 made provision for local authorities to give improvement grants and intermediate grants which would help families, including disabled people, wanting to adapt their own homes. For more information see

Chapter 8; details of the grants can be obtained from the local authority within which the person lives.

Social services departments provide adaptations to disabled people's homes under the Chronically Sick and Disabled Persons Act 1970 and these range from simple handrails to complete bathroom/toilet extensions and stairlifts. Most social services departments financially assess the disabled person and require a contribution towards the cost of more major adaptations. Handrails and other small works may be provided free of charge. Disability has to be permanent and substantial to qualify.

The social services worker who encounters a disabled person with acute housing problems will consider the two alternatives of adaptation or rehousing very carefully, and it will help to have some understanding of the scope of these alternatives.

Adaptations

There are some reasons for preferring this alternative:

1. The person wants to stay where he is for various reasons; acceptance of neighbours, for example, or supportive help nearby.
2. His house or flat is basically of the right size, shape and dimensions for the family needs, in the number of bedrooms, layout, etc.
3. There are only one or two major problems within the house: for instance, the kitchen surfaces are not accessible, the main staircase cannot be negotiated, or the person is unable to get into the bath.
4. The total cost of adapting the house to make it suitable will not be so exorbitant as to make it prohibitive; that is, it is within the means of housing or social services departments and the client's assessed contribution towards the work. (In order to make some houses suitable so much work would have to be done as to amount to totally redesigning and rebuilding the property.)
5. The extent of the building work required during adaptation will not be totally disruptive to the family's life so as to make it positively harmful to their well-being. (In some local authority owned houses it may be possible to move the family out into temporary accommodation for

a period to enable the work to be done. This may be considered a possibility where the previous reasons apply and where there is no more suitable property available for local rehousing.)

Types of adaptations

The advice of an occupational therapist will be required and it will be necessary for her to visit the disabled person to assess the type and feasibility of adaptations. In many social services departments occupational therapists are employed and will usually take over the practical work of the case from the social worker when adaptations are to be made, although the social worker may continue to be involved with the family. The occupational therapist will discuss with the disabled person the difficulties which he is having and set out some proposals which are acceptable to him and his family. She will visit the house with an architect or surveyor who will then work out the adaptations in more detail and prepare a drawing of the work. At this stage every detail will be carefully considered with the family to ensure that nothing important has been overlooked.

Some adaptations have already been suggested in Chapter 15. Here are other adaptations which might be proposed:

1. Approach ramps to front and back door (minimum gradient 1 in 12 and minimum width 1,000 mm). Level platform is required at the top of a ramp (minimum dimensions 1,000 mm wide and 1,200 mm long). Surface should be slip resistant.
2. Remove thresholds to front door and other doors within the house where they exist.
3. Rehang any door to facilitate manoeuvre with either walking aid or wheelchair.
4. Widen doorways (minimum clear opening of 770 mm desirable).
5. Fit sliding doors if necessary and when possible.
6. Fit suitable door controls (D-handles and lever handles are easier to manage than door knobs).
7. Kitchen alterations. A continuous sequence of units, worktop/sink/worktop/cooker/worktop is usually most convenient for food preparation. Provision might be made for work to be done from a seated position –

pull-out boards below fixed work surfaces can be useful.

8. Rearrangement of kitchen storage.
9. Alteration to sink unit to enable a disabled person to sit with legs under.
10. Provision of lever taps.
11. Provision of overhead track hoist in bedroom.
12. Provision of shower cubicle in bedroom.
13. Alteration to toilet – relocation of pan – provision of handrails.
14. Installation of another toilet in the house (e.g. under the stairs) when the existing one is totally inaccessible.
15. Alteration to bathroom to allow for better use of space by disabled person, e.g. change bath to sit-up type, replace bath with shower, or install a shower over the bath. Install overhead track hoist in the bathroom.
16. Build bathroom/shower/toilet extension.
17. Install stairslift or vertical home lift.
18. Alteration to electric sockets, change of position for easier reach, additional sockets where needed.
19. Provision of extra lighting where needed.
20. Provision of central heating.

Rehousing

Rehousing will be considered when the disabled person's accommodation is totally unsuitable for him with his disability and impossible to adapt to satisfy all his requirements. For example, the paraplegic man in a wheelchair who returns from hospital to live alone in a second floor flat. The doorways and passageways are too narrow to take his wheelchair, and the kitchen and bathroom are too small to accommodate him in the chair. In this example, the man would be isolated and helpless and rehousing is the only solution. If he is not already a council tenant he will need to become a housing applicant; otherwise he will apply for a transfer. Most local housing authorities operate a medical points system and give some priority to cases which are urgent for medical reasons. Housing associations also accept nominations from local housing authorities and therefore there may be some choice as to where people can be more suitably housed.

Local authorities accept the Department of the Environment categorisation of housing for the disabled and make provision of the three types of housing for disabled and elderly people.

These are:

(*a*) specially designed wheelchair housing;
(*b*) mobility housing;
(*c*) sheltered housing.

Wheelchair housing

The concept of wheelchair housing was introduced by the Department of the Environment in 1975 and differs considerably from general-purpose housing standards. It is most often found in single-storey construction (the bungalow) and in ground floor flats. Many of these units have been built by local authorities and housing associations all over the country and have been found to be most successful when they are integrated into a scheme of normal housing. This is because the disabled person can then be integrated into a normal community close to general amenities such as shops and banks. Where the wheelchair housing has been built as an isolated special development, a ghetto-like feeling has arisen and such developments are often hotbeds of bitterness, bickering and resentment.

The special features of wheelchair housing are that "space standards are based on a general expectation that the number of people occupying a wheelchair dwelling will be one less than the designated size" (D. of E. HDD, paper 2/75) and that easy access is provided for a wheelchair to all rooms, which enables the wheelchair user to operate freely within them. There are very many particular dimensions which have to be incorporated and these can be referred to in Selwyn Goldsmith's book, *Designing for the Disabled* (item no. 46 in the Bibliography).

Mobility housing

The concept of mobility housing was introduced by the Department of the Environment in 1974 and was devised so that "authorities have dwellings more readily available for disabled people without having to go in for major adaptations or to wait until new accommodation can be built". It was intended to make ordinary housing more convenient for physically handicapped people and to cater for all ambulant disabled people with or without walking aids, as well as those who use wheel-chairs but are able to stand to transfer, and move a few steps, if need be, with something to hold on to. So it can be seen that by building all ground floor accommodation to mobility housing standards, it can be ensured that a disabled person living in one flat will be able to visit all the others at ground level, and elderly people will be able to continue living on in a flat if they become increasingly infirm and physically handicapped as they grow older.

1. The entrance must have a ramped or level approach and a flush threshold.
2. Entrances and principal rooms (living room, dining room, kitchen and at least one bedroom) must have 900 mm doorsets, and passageways serving these rooms must be at least 900 mm wide.
3. Bathroom and WC must be at the same level as the entrance.

Most local authorities have adopted the mobility housing concept for their newly built properties, so that much suitable ground floor accommodation is now available.

Sheltered housing

This is the term given to housing which is built specially for elderly and disabled people and makes provision for some kind of supervision, usually in the form of a warden who lives on the premises. Tenants of sheltered flats have their own front door but are able to call for help through a call system when they need it. Most sheltered housing is built to mobility housing standards and some to wheelchair housing standards. For elderly and disabled people who wish to retain their independence, this is a very useful alternative to living in an institution.

Rehousing and adaptation

Having considered the possibilities of both adaptations and rehousing, there is a third possibility combining the two. This solution gives local authorities the opportunity to build up their stock of housing units suitable for the disabled and elderly population by adapting existing council houses to mobility housing standards as they become vacant, and housing disabled people on the waiting list in them. This is most easily done through the housing rehabilitation programme, in housing action areas and general improvement areas, when work is being done to bring old property up to a modern standard.

The social services worker will be aware that there are many competing claims for houses in any community and the disabled person takes his place amongst the housing problems of homeless families, elderly people, single parent families and all those who wish to live in a low rise housing. The needs of the disabled are just as urgent as all of these and worthy of a considered housing policy.

PART FOUR

Provision for physically handicapped people

20 Rehabilitation centres

Rehabilitation when applied to physically handicapped people means restoration of the person to his fullest physical, mental and social capability. This will also imply the maintenance of his maximum function. The areas of rehabilitation will therefore be:

(a) medical and/or surgical treatment including the relief of pain;
(b) psychological adjustment and motivation;
(c) activites of self-care;
(d) financial livelihood;
(e) housing;
(f) transport;
(g) occupation – including employment, sheltered work, housework, educational and voluntary work;
(h) recreation;
(i) sexual activity.

Hospital rehabilitation

Most acute hospitals and many long-stay hospitals nowadays recognise the importance of a complete rehabilitation programme which will start in hospital and continue in the community when the patient is discharged. For rehabilitation to be really successful it has to start early, that is, soon after the person is admitted to hospital, as it is important to prevent the complications of bed rest. Stephen Mattingly in *Rehabilitation Today* (item no. 25 in the Bibliography) describes the scope of rehabilitation as follows:

"The aim is to minimise a patient's disability by:

Preventing complications of bed rest	such as bedsores, urinary infections, renal stones, venous thrombosis, muscle wasting, joint stiffness, and contractures by good nursing, physiotherapy and early mobilisation;
Restoring the patient's physical and mental health	as far as possible by drugs, remedial exercise, speech therapy, functional activities (such as walking, writing, cooking, and other household tasks) and work therapy;
Providing aids and appliances	to compensate for loss of function, especially mobility (including crutches, calipers, surgical shoes, special clothing, personal aids, artificial limbs and wheelchairs);
Resettlement at home	including home nursing, loan of aids, adaptations, telephones, home helps, meals-on-wheels, residential and day centres;
Resettlement in work	in open industry or sheltered workshops following negotiations with employer, visit to jobcentre or employment office, occupational assessment or vocational training."

Rehabilitation in hospital centres round the treatment team of doctor, nurse, physiotherapist, occupational therapist, speech therapist and social worker, and even if rehabilitation is not focussed in a special unit or department the team is still present and must co-ordinate its work to achieve the most satisfactory results with the patient. Much good rehabilitation work is carried out even in dilapidated buildings because the team has a unified, co-ordinated approach.

Many hospitals have rehabilitation units which specialise in the rehabilitation of particular types of disability; for example, some specialise in the rehabilitation of patients following head injuries and neurological diseases, some in rehabilitation following strokes and some in the assessment and rehabilitation of very severely disabled patients. Other specialist rehabilitation units are separate but attached to hospitals, such as the spinal injuries units. Social work staff are advised to familiarise themselves with local facilities for rehabilitation.

All-important is the transition of the patient from the hospital to the community, for he may be able to function independently in a well-designed and suitably protected hospital environment only to find that he becomes dependent when faced with physical and psychological constraints at home. Therefore, realistic rehabilitation will take into account his home and social background and discharge plans will begin at a very early stage in the rehabilitation programme. The patient and his family should ideally be considered to be the most vital members of the rehabilitation team.

Home rehabilitation

Much of this book is about rehabilitation at home. All of the areas of rehabilitation listed at the beginning of this chapter are those which the social worker investigates when she is allocated a physically handicapped client at home. This investigation will involve liaison with other members of the treatment team in the community who are often unaware of each other's involvement with the patient. The social worker will often have the task of co-ordinating the work of members of this team and facilitating communication between them. The community team will usually include the family doctor, district nurse and occupational therapist but will also include other community staff such as the home help, family aide, Disablement Resettlement Officer and Careers Officer. The Housing Medical Officer may also become involved where alternative accommodation is required.

Co-ordinated rehabilitation is far more difficult to manage in the community, where staff are working in geographical separation from one another and may be employed by different agencies. It is a concept which warrants further study, for it avoids the upheaval and expense of hospital admission and may be much more effective in maintaining physically handicapped people in their own homes. Hospital-at-home and home care projects are recent developments and have yet to be evaluated against hospital admissions. Such projects may require separate facilities in the community for more intensive rehabilitation. A short-stay residential home or a training flat, perhaps attached to a day centre, would provide a setting for more intensive practice in independent daily living, particularly for young people or for the elderly who may need to concentrate the mind upon independence away from their own home, with its constraints of family and a familiar pattern of dependence.

Medical Rehabilitation Centres

Medical Rehabilitation Centres have been set up to provide intensive rehabilitation of people who are seriously handicapped by injury or disease. They provide a progression from the local rehabilitation unit to a more intensive regime of treatment, a "finishing school" in many cases. Most centres are residential and the average length of stay is six weeks, although some people may require a longer period at the centre. Referral is made by the hospital consultant, or the GP if the person is not attending a hospital. Children under 16 are not normally admitted to residential medical rehabilitation centres and people over 70 may not be fit enough to benefit from intensive rehabilitation.

The Medical Rehabilitation Centre offers:

(*a*) an expert assessment of disability and its effect upon the individual's independence at home and at work;
(*b*) a practical test of functional activities such as walking, driving and use of public transport;
(*c*) intensive treatment as often as is required to strengthen weak muscles and mobilise stiff joints;
(*d*) retraining in such activities of daily living as dressing, washing, eating and the cooking and preparation of food;
(*e*) provision of suitable aids such as sticks, calipers, hoists and wheelchairs; people requiring personal transport may be assessed for their ability to drive hand-controlled vehicles.

In addition, many centres assess communication problems, with the aid of speech therapists and occupational therapists and attempt to retrain the person in speaking and writing. Almost all centres provide some form of work assessment to establish whether the disabled worker is employable and, if so, whether he can return to his previous job or must be resettled, possibly after vocational training. The special employment rehabilitation services are described in the next chapter.

Patients each have a daily treatment programme and are progressed from individual to group treatment, from remedial therapy to work assessment. They are discussed at regular weekly case conferences attended by medical and remedial staff, the social worker and the Disablement Resettlement Officer (DRO). On his leaving the Centre a report on the person is sent to his referring doctor and copies may be sent to the local authority social services department and to the local DRO. No one medical rehabilitation centre is exactly like another. The main MRCs are listed below to provide some idea of the variations.

London and south-eastern and southern England

Medical Rehabilitation Centre, Camden Road, London NW1
This is a day centre with no residential accommodation although a few patients can be accommodated in local hotels within reach of the centre. The centre treats mainly men with orthopaedic conditions but also accepts women, and people with arthritis, strokes and other medical conditions. Work resettlement is part of the programme.

Garston Manor Rehabilitation Centre, High Elms Lane, Garston, Herts
A unit with 65 beds, this centre receives patients from all areas of the United Kingdom, but most come from south-east England. Garston Manor is an MRC with an Employment Rehabilitation Centre in the same grounds. People with a wide variety of disabilities receive medical and/or industrial rehabilitation.

Farnham Park Rehabilitation Centre, Farnham Royal, Slough, Bucks
With a catchment area of the whole of the United Kingdom and overseas, Farnham Park has 65 beds and takes 40 out-patients a day. This centre caters particularly for people whose work or other activities, including sport, demands a high degree of physical fitness.

Mary Marlborough Lodge, Nuffield Orthopaedic Centre, Headington, Oxford
All ages including children are catered for at this 18-bedded unit. It is a disabled living research unit specialising in the assessment of very severely disabled people. There is also a two-bedded flat for training the person and a relative or companion, or a disabled

couple. The average length of stay is two to three weeks and one-day assessments can be arranged.

Rivermead Rehabilitation Hospital, Abingdon Road, Oxford
This 50-bedded unit caters for people with a wide range of disabilities but has always specialised in rehabilitation of people with brain damage as a result of injury, infection and surgery. Patients often have behavioural and intellectual problems as well as their physical disability. A small number of very severely handicapped patients are admitted for assessment. Rivermead's catchment area is the whole of the United Kingdom and overseas.

Passmore Edwards Rehabilitation Centre, Clacton-on-Sea, Essex
With 77 beds this centre accommodates for rehabilitation those people requiring minimal nursing care. A very small number of very severely disabled people can be admitted at any one time. The catchment area is the whole of the United Kingdom. There is a flat for retraining in independent living.

Princess Mary's Hospital, Margate, Kent
This unit mainly takes referrals from hospitals in the South East Thames Regional Health Authority. It has 194 beds and rehabilitates people with a variety of conditions, including colostomy and ileostomy and following heart surgery. The average length of stay is three weeks but severely disabled people may stay for several months.

Rehabilitation Centre, Oldstock Hospital, Salisbury, Wilts
Oldstock provides a local and regional service. Rehabilitation includes industrial assessment and there are links with the local day school for handicapped children, local firms and the social services sheltered workshop which is in the hospital grounds. A local employer's association co-operates directly with the unit. There are 24 beds.

Wolfson MRC, Copse Hill, Wimbledon, London SW20
With residential accommodation for 48 patients and another 50 day patients, this centre specialises in the rehabilitation of people with severe neurological disabilities. It takes referrals from all areas of the United Kingdom and overseas.

Joint Services MRC, RAF Chessington, Surrey
The centre has 200 beds for people from the three Services suffering from orthopaedic and post-traumatic conditions. There are also 40 beds for those servicemen with severe handicaps resulting from head injuries and neurological diseases. As well as the usual remedial treatments, this centre has an education section and workshops to assess and train people in mechanical skills appropriate to the

Forces. A small number of NHS patients are admitted but this hospital is mainly for servicemen of non-commissioned ranks.

Medical Rehabilitation Unit, RAF Headley Court, Epsom, Surrey
Similar to RAF Chessington, this 104-bedded unit takes senior NCOs and officers from the three Services.

East Anglia

Mundesley Rehabilitation Unit, Mundesley Hospital, Mundesley, Norfolk
With 60 beds, this unit takes referrals from local hospitals of people with a variety of conditions, including colostomy and ileostomy.

Midlands and northern England

Cedars Rehabilitation Unit, Cedars Hospital, Nottingham
Referrals to this 14-bedded unit are mainly from the surrounding area. Most residential patients go home at the weekends. There are also up to 80 out-patients daily and most disabling conditions are treated.

Etwall Rehabilitation Unit, Etwall Hospital, Etwall, Derbyshire
People are mainly admitted from Derby, Nottingham and Lincolnshire. There are 94 beds and patients are usually referred from acute hospitals at an early stage in their treatment. Thirty out-patients also attend daily and some patients may spend part of each day at Long Eaton Employment Rehabilitation Centre nearby.

Whitehaven Rehabilitation Centre, Whitehaven Hospital, Whitehaven, Cumbria
Originally a rehabilitation department for injured miners, this is now a new rehabilitation centre. Twenty-five day patients attend the centre and some beds are available for people from further afield. The catchment area is mainly West Cumbria.

Scotland

Rehabilitation Unit, Bridge of Earn Hospital, Perthshire
This 95-bedded unit takes referrals from Scotland, northern England and Northern Ireland. People admitted have to be able to dress, wash and feed themselves and get to the rehabilitation unit, a hundred yards from the residential accommodation. A very small number of severely handicapped people in wheelchairs can be accepted.

Medical Rehabilitation Unit, 90 Bellshill Road, Uddington, Lanarkshire
With a catchment area of Lanarkshire, Glasgow, Renfrew and Dunbartonshire, the centre takes people with a wide range of disabilities.

There is no residential accommodation but the centre takes 180 day patients. It is near to Bellshill Employment Rehabilitation Centre for industrial rehabilitation.

21 Employment services

Disabled people often experience difficulty in finding employment. Inevitably, any disability rules out some forms of employment for the disabled person and therefore job opportunities are more limited than they are for the able-bodied. In addition to the specific disability, the difficulties of travel to work, access to buildings and using amenities such as toilets and canteens, and prejudice on the part of the able-bodied, do much to keep the disabled out of work.

In recognition of these difficulties, the government has set up various schemes to further employment opportunities for handicapped people. Successive governments since the war have passed legislation, have provided advice, support and training for handicapped people and have spent a good deal of money in publicity schemes to try to persuade employers to employ more disabled workers. The Department of Employment's Manpower Services Commission has delegated the job of finding work for the disabled to its Employment Service Agency, alongside the services for the able-bodied. The Training Services Agency incorporates schemes for training the disabled for work both within and outside its Training Opportunities Scheme (TOPS). The legislation is dealt with in Chapter 8, the remainder of this chapter being taken up with a description of the employment services for disabled people.

Registration as a disabled person

Under the terms of the Disabled Persons Employment Act 1944, disabled people may apply to be registered with the Department of Employment. It should be noted that the register kept by the Department of Employment is not the same as the register maintained by the local authorities, which is described in Chapter 10, even though the same people may sometimes be on both. The handicapped person who wishes to be registered for employment should apply to the Disablement Resettlement Officer (DRO) at the local Employment Office or Jobcentre. The DRO may need to see a doctor's certificate if the disability is not an obvious one, and he will need to satisfy himself that the disabled person is capable of working, is available for work and is likely to remain disabled for at least twelve months. Upon registration, the disabled person will be given a certificate known as the "green card", which he or she can show to employers. The green card can be issued for periods of up to ten years, after which it can still be renewed if the person is still disabled and is still available for work. Disabled people do not have to be registered with the Department of Employment, but several important concessions are available only to those who have done so. These benefits are as follows:

1. Employers of more than twenty workers have a duty to employ disabled workers totalling three per cent of the workforce. Only the registered may be counted (see Chapter 8).
2. Certain jobs – currently car park attendants and passenger lift attendants – are designated solely for registered disabled people.
3. Admission to most sheltered workshops (but not local authority work centres – see p. 215) is restricted to the registered.
4. Aids to employment and fares to work are only given to green card holders.

There is quite a lot of resistance to registration among handicapped people. Those whose handicap is not too obvious say that it is a disadvantage to be known to be disabled. Many job application forms ask if the applicant is a registered disabled person and some people have found that it is an advantage to be able to answer "no" to that question. Although prejudice undoubtedly does exist among employers (and workers too) it may well be that a conscientious employer trying to fill his three per cent quota might prefer to engage a mildly disabled person out of several applicants. Other disabled people who are already employed may not want the stigma of disability made official and therefore do not register. As no one can be compelled to register, it might be as well for those professionally involved with disability to regard registration as a service to be taken up if required rather than a duty which every disabled person of employable age ought to perform.

Disabled people in open employment

The majority of known handicapped workers are employed in open occupations. Almost a million are working at jobs alongside the able-bodied, compared with the 14,000 in sheltered employment (see below). Some have found jobs for themselves and others who were already employed before becoming disabled have been retained by or redeployed within their own firm. For those who are not able to find work on their own there are several government-sponsored services which can help them to become employed.

The Employment Service Agency employs some 500 Disablement Resettlement Officers (DROs) at employment offices throughout the country. (Under an experimental scheme a few are employed attached to hospitals.) There are also sixty senior DROs. DROs are specially trained to help the disabled to find suitable jobs, to assess the type of work they can do and to help employers who wish to employ handicapped people. A good DRO will know the types of jobs available in his or her own area. He or she will be known to individual businessmen and managers and will have gained their confidence in his or her ability to provide good workers and to help them to settle into employment. DROs work very closely with medical and social services and are very important members of the rehabilitation team. All disabled persons seeking help with work problems should go and see their DRO. (Blind people use the Blind Persons' Resettlement Officer, BPRO.)

At the DRO's request, the Employment Service Agency can provide special aids to employment so as to enable the disabled worker to do his job effectively. Machines can be adapted for one-hand control, special seats can be provided for those with back problems, flashing light signals can replace warning buzzers for the deaf, and braille devices can be provided for the blind. Certain adaptations to buildings may be paid for by the Department of Employment on the DRO's recommendation. Where necessary, on-the-job training can be arranged with no loss to the employer.

Also arranged by the DRO are some services for the very severely disabled worker. Those who cannot use public transport and who cannot drive themselves can be given three-quarters of the cost of taxi fares to work up to a limit of £25 per week (or £5 per day for those who do not work full-time). Extra costs other than taxi fares can be considered on their individual merits. People receiving Mobility Allowance can still be helped if they are unable to drive because of age or disability, or if their vehicle is temporarily off the road.

Employment Rehabilitation Centres

When someone has been away from work due to illness, injury or even long unemployment, he or she may need to attend an employment rehabilitation centre. The Employment Service Agency maintains a network of 26 Employment Rehabilitation Centres spread throughout the country (these are not the same as Medical Rehabilitation Centres). The purpose of such centres is to accustom the person to normal working conditions again and to assess the potential for paid employment.

Most of these centres are near to Skillcentres or to other factories so as to give an atmosphere of real work. Most of them are non-residential and workers come to work every day and work normal hours. The centres are run on normal factory and business lines and accept contracts for work from local firms and government departments. Types of work done include assembly work, machine operating, clerical and business work and some heavy manual labour.

Centres provide individual programmes for each person attending. During the first week, the manager consults with the medical officer, the DRO, the psychiatrist and social worker if necessary, and then decides what work the disabled person should be given to do and how long he should stay at the centre. Most people stay for six weeks, but the rehabilitation period can be much longer if necessary. The rehabilitee's progress is assessed at intervals throughout his stay and at the end of the programme definite recommendations for employment will be made. At the moment, two-thirds of the people who have passed through such centres are finding work or places on training courses within three months of completion of the rehabilitation.

The Employment Service Agency can arrange for people to attend rehabilitation centres run by voluntary bodies, and can pay all the necessary fees and allowances. Blind persons can attend the Royal National Institute for the Blind rehabilitation centre at Torquay. There are also special voluntarily run centres for spastics run by the Spastics Society.

Clients of Employment Rehabilitation Centres are paid maintenance allowances which are slightly higher than unemployment or sickness benefit, and they are credited with National Insurance contributions. Free mid-day meals are provided and those who have to leave home to attend are paid lodgings allowances. For some, a job rehearsal is arranged towards the end of the rehabilitation period. The employee is paid the allowances as usual while he or she tries out a job with an employer. This scheme allows both employer and employee to see if the worker is fit to work, without the employer being committed to keeping on the worker who is not up to it.

Training for employment

Disabled people often find that, though capable of some sorts of work, they cannot return to the same employment that they were in before becoming disabled. When this is the case the DRO will often arrange for them to train alongside the able-bodied on a course run or sponsored by the Training Opportunities Scheme, or TOPS, as it is generally known.

TOPS is run by the Training Services Agency part of the Manpower Services Commission, and is intended to provide opportunities to train for a wide variety of skilled manual and clerical occupations. Any person of working age may apply to train, even if already employed. People leaving the Armed Forces often use this advantage to train for a new career. Acceptance on a given course depends upon aptitudes and qualifications. All training under TOPS is free to the trainee and a training allowance and National Insurance contributions will be paid. Where necessary lodgings allowances are made, and lunches are free; travelling expenses are provided for those who need them.

The Training Services Agency runs several Skillcentres (formerly known as Government Training Centres) which teach a variety of skilled and semi-skilled occupations. The courses being run reflect the demands of the economy, so that

213

trainees are likely to get a job when they leave. Courses run from six to nine months and the sort of subjects available include clerical, business and administrative studies, engineering trades of various kinds, electrical work, construction trades, and radio and television repairing. Disabled people who are able to work at these trades may enrol on these courses and do so beside able-bodied trainees.

Also under the TOPS scheme, disabled people who need special facilities may go to one of the special colleges run by voluntary bodies. While they are there they will receive all the usual allowances and have their fees paid by the Department of Employment. There are four colleges for the physically handicapped that are often used under the scheme: St Loye's, Exeter, Finchale in Durham, Portland Training College near Mansfield, Nottingham, and Queen Elizabeth Training College in Leatherhead, Surrey. These colleges offer further education in general school subjects as well as tuition in clerical work, engineering trades and carpentry. There is also Banstead Place, a centre for the assessment and further education of school leavers with severe physical handicaps. The average length of stay is between six and twelve months and there is accommodation for about 30 people. Students are sponsored by their local authority. Blind students may attend the Royal National Institute for the Blind or Royal National College for the Blind training courses in typing, telephony, piano tuning and computer programming. There is also a Training Services Agency Skillcentre for the blind at Letchworth which offers tuition in assembly work and light engineering.

The Training Services Agency may pay the costs of trainees and students attending courses run by universities and other colleges of higher education, if there are good reasons for attending such courses and if grants are not available from the local education authority. This is known as the Professional Training Scheme. Disabled students who are suitably qualified may be trained under the scheme and it is especially suitable for those who have to leave their usual profession because of disability. For example, a schoolteacher good at art who was becoming deaf might train as a commercial artist and an athletics coach losing his or her sight might train to become a physiotherapist.

Finally, it should be remembered that the Department of

Employment can give a grant of £30 per week to an employer who accepts an employee to train on the job, under the Training with Employers Scheme. In such cases, the employer must agree to take the employee on to his payroll and to continue to employ him for at least a year after completion of training. Disabled people are eligible for training under this scheme, and should apply through the DRO, if they wish to take advantage of its arrangements.

The handicapped school leaver

All local education authorities must employ careers officers who can advise school leavers on the sort of jobs they might be able to enter. Many authorities employ a specialist careers officer for the handicapped, but all Careers Officers (formerly known as Youth Employment Officers) can begin to advise the handicapped child while he is still at school, and even before he or she has decided which subjects to study for GCE and CSE. Careers Officers work very closely with schools and with the medical and social services when necessary. Handicapped school leavers may seek help from either the Careers Officer or the DRO.

Sheltered employment

Some handicapped people are not capable of working to the standards expected of employees in open industry. Though able to do useful work, they may be very slow, or may need time off for a lot of medical treatment. Some may be very good quick workers but have epileptic fits so often that they would not be accepted by an employer. Some discharged mental patients may need to be given special understanding because of their behavioural problems. In such cases, employment in a sheltered workshop can allow the disabled person to do useful work and take home a reasonable wage. Any disabled person wishing to work in sheltered employment should apply to the DRO, who will arrange for the case to be considered by the nearest suitable establishment. The sheltered workshops are not owned by the Employment Service Agency and set their own criteria for acceptance. The Blind Persons Resettlement Officer arranges sheltered work for the blind, and for those partially sighted people whose sight is likely to deteriorate.

Sheltered workshops may be owned by local authorities, by

215

voluntary bodies or by Remploy, which though government-owned is allowed to manage its own day-to-day affairs. Almost all sheltered workshops operate at a loss, and some at an enormous loss. Only a handful break even and a mere two or three make a profit. Local authorities are responsible for the fees necessary to place a disabled person in a voluntary work-shop, though they may claim a refund from the government. (Any Remploy losses are made up from central government funds.)

The sort of work available in sheltered workshops varies greatly. Some places are still turning out the traditional crafts of basketry, brush making and mat weaving, even though these trades have long since ceased to make a profit, even for the able-bodied. More modern workshops accept contracts for assembly work and packaging. Some make their own brands of goods such as soaps, shampoos, textiles, leather goods, bedding and furniture. Employees in sheltered workshops work the normal working week and their wages are usually agreed upon with the appropriate trade unions.

Those professionally involved with disabled people need to be aware of the services which exist to help them find work. It should never be forgotten, however, that finding the right job is almost always going to be difficult – and much more difficult than it is for able-bodied people. Despite legislation and a good deal of government publicity, there is still a lot of prejudice about. Disabled people are less able to be switched around between buildings and less able to move about the country in search of employment. Therefore they are more likely to become redundant than their able-bodied workmates, and in periods of unemployment they are heavily over-rep-resented in the unemployment statistics. The disabled person who is looking for work will need a lot of support and en-couragement from those working with him, and doctors and social workers need to go out of their way to bolster self-confidence in disabled people in this situation.

22 Welfare rights and social security benefits

There is a wide variety of benefits, pensions, allowances and grants from the Department of Health and Social Security designed to cover all situations in which a person suffers from low income (or no income at all), or where he may have extra financial outlay, because of illness, disability or some other disadvantage. The current rates payable are set out on DHSS leaflet FB 1, *Family Benefits and Pensions*, which is up-dated in November each year. Because of the constant changes in the amount of money that can be paid, actual figures are not given in this book. The aim of this chapter is to describe the main benefits for which handicapped people are likely to be eligible so that they or their social workers will have some idea of the help that can be given.

Benefits for handicapped children

Child benefit

All children, handicapped or not, attract child benefit. This weekly payment replaces the old family allowance and was designed to help offset the expense of rearing a family. It is paid usually to the mother, but it can be paid to a lone father or to a relative or guardian who is looking after a child. Higher rates can be paid to single parents with very low incomes. It is non-contributory, not means tested and not taxed. People wishing to claim child benefit should complete form CH 2, obtainable from any social security office.

Attendance allowance

Handicapped children become eligible for this at the age of two. It is designed to help handicapped people of all ages to get the care and attention they need. Claimants must be severely physically or mentally handicapped (including deaf or blind children) *and* require a lot of looking after by day and/ or night for at least six months. There are two rates: a higher one for those needing help by day and by night, and a lower one for those needing help by day or by night. Attendance allowance is non-contributory, not means tested and not taxed. Handicapped people or parents of a handicapped child can apply on the form in leaflet NI 205, obtainable from a social security office.

Invalid care allowance

This allowance is designed to compensate people who cannot go to work because they are looking after a relative who is receiving attendance allowance. Those caring for handicapped children may be eligible if they are men or single women of working age. Married women who are living with their husbands are not eligible, even if they would otherwise have returned to work. As most handicapped children are living with their parents, very few of them have relatives who can claim; however, this allowance is very useful to single-parent families as it includes additions for other dependants. Invalid care allowance is non-contributory and not means tested but it is taxable. It can be claimed using the form in leaflet NI 212, obtainable from social security offices.

Mobility allowance

People between the age of five and retirement age who are unable to walk and likely to remain so for twelve months can be given a mobility allowance. This allowance was designed to prevent the more severely disabled from being prisoners in their own homes, and the parents of handicapped children from experiencing the difficulties of a child who couldn't be taken out. It is not paid to deaf or blind people, as they can be taken out or go out on their own, but people who are deaf *and* blind may apply. It has occasionally been paid to mentally handicapped children whose behaviour problems prevent their being taken on public vehicles. People who receive mobility allowance may spend it how they like, but it is really intended to pay taxi fares or to help towards the cost of buying and running a car. Parents who do not own a car can arrange to pay their allowance to the charity Motability in return for the lease of a car (for further details, see p. 223 below).

Mobility allowance belongs to the handicapped person and goes with him wherever he goes, be it home, hospital, boarding school, foster home or so on. It is non-contributory and not means tested but it is taxable. Parents of a handicapped child can apply on his behalf using the form in leaflet NI 211 from social security offices.

Free milk

Handicapped children between the ages of 5 and 16 who are not attending school for some reason are entitled to seven pints of milk free per week. (Children in special schools do not have to pay for their milk.) Free milk is non-contributory, not means tested and not taken into account for tax purposes. It can be claimed on form FW 20 from social security offices.

Extra assistance for parents of a handicapped child who are receiving Supplementary Benefit

Parents on Supplementary Benefit may be able to claim extra allowances if a child needs a special diet, special clothing or extra heating and laundry. If the child needs frequent visits to hospital, parents may be able to get help with fares if they show their order book to the hospital social worker.

The Family Fund

Though not a social security benefit, it is logical to mention this fund here. The fund was set up at government request, and is administered by the Joseph Rowntree Memorial Trust. It aims to provide grants of money, goods and services to families with a severely handicapped child if the need cannot be met from normal government or social services funds. The sort of services the fund has provided include telephone installation for the parents of a child subject to sudden illnesses, washing machines for incontinent teenagers and driving lessons for mothers of disabled children. It can also help with holidays. Applications can be made to The Secretary, The Family Fund, Joseph Rowntree Memorial Trust, Beverley, House, Shipton Road, York, YO3 6RB.

Benefits for disabled people of working age who are not working

Sickness benefit

Sickness benefit is part of the national insurance scheme under which people who have paid contributions when working can draw benefit for up to 28 weeks when they are unable to work through sickness or injury. It includes an earnings-related supplement and extra benefit for dependants. This benefit is contributory, but not means tested or taxed.

Persons wishing to claim should visit their doctor to obtain a doctor's statement (formerly a doctor's certificate) which on completion should be sent to the local social security office within six days of becoming unable to work.

Invalidity benefit

A person who is still ill or disabled after 28 weeks of receiving sickness benefit will transfer to invalidity benefit if his doctor finds him still unable to work. Invalidity benefit payments are slightly higher than sickness benefits.

Invalidity benefit is made up of a basic invalidity pension, which includes provision for dependants, plus invalidity allowance for those who become chronically sick or disabled below the ages of 60 (men) or 55 (women). Higher rates are paid to those incapacitated early in life. The benefit is contributory, but it is not means tested and is not taxed. It is claimed on a doctor's statement in the same way as sickness benefit.

Non-contributory invalidity pension

Men and single women of working age who have not paid sufficient (or indeed any) national insurance contributions, and who become unable to work because of sickness or injury for at least six months, may be entitled to non-contributory invalidity pension. Rates of payment are quite a lot less than those given under the contributory scheme though there will still be additions for dependants. Lower rates are paid to people receiving other benefits. Married women cannot claim this unless they are also unable to perform all or almost all normal household duties.

Non-contributory invalidity pension is means tested but not taxed. It should be claimed using the form in leaflet NI

210 (or NI 214 for married women), obtainable from social security offices.

Industrial injury benefit

People who are unable to work following an industrial accident or because of some occupational disease caught at work are eligible for this benefit. Payments are slightly higher than those of sickness benefit and they include an earnings-related supplement and additions for dependants. Benefits are payable for up to 26 weeks, after which the claimant, if still incapacitated, will be invited to transfer to Industrial Disablement Benefit.

People receiving industrial injury benefit cannot receive sickness benefit as well. It is non-contributory, not means tested and not taxed. People who wish to claim should report the accident or illness to their employers at once and obtain a doctor's statement, which they should send to the local social security office within six days.

Industrial disablement benefit

People who are disabled because of industrial disease or accidents at work may be eligible for industrial disablement benefit. If still unable to work when industrial injury benefit ceases they are usually sent a claim form direct from the social security office. A medical board decides the form and amount of payment to be made in each case. People with less severe disabilities will be granted a lump sum payment, while those more seriously incapacitated will be granted a weekly pension. Extra-high rates are paid to those who are unable to return to their former work or who need constant attendance, or who become unemployable. People who are able to return to work may still receive industrial disability benefit if they retain some permanent impairment.

This benefit is non-contributory, not means tested and not taxed. If claim forms are not sent automatically they can be requested from a social security office.

War disablement pension

This is paid to persons disabled as a result of active service in both world wars or since the Second World War. It is also payable to civilians disabled by enemy action in the Second World War. The level of payment is decided by the degree of disability and the rank held in the services. It includes additions for dependants and for special handicaps. Payments are usually higher than the equivalent national insurance benefits, and they are not affected by earnings and other benefits to which the pensioner subsequently becomes entitled. (A war pensioner who can still work also receives sickness benefit if he is away ill.)

War disablement pension is non-contributory, is not means tested and is not taxed. Claims can be made on a form obtained from the nearest social security office.

Supplementary benefit

This is the safety net of the welfare state. People over sixteen years who are not working full time and who do not have enough money to live on can be paid supplementary benefit even if some of their needs are already being met by some other payment. (It is often used to "top up" an old age pension, when it is called supplementary pension.) Disabled people who have never been able to work and who have never contributed to the national insurance scheme often derive their basic income from this.

Amounts paid vary considerably, as both income and outgoings are taken into account when rates are being decided for each person. The value of the house lived in and a certain amount of capital are ignored, though savings above this figure result in a proportionate reduction in benefits. Sick and disabled people can be paid higher rates if they need special diets, special clothing, extra heating or a lot of laundry. Blind people are entitled to higher rates as well.

People receiving supplementary benefit are automatically entitled to exemption from National Health Service charges, should they require treatment. They do not have to pay for prescriptions, dental treatment, spectacles (always assuming that they consent to be seen in NHS frames) or surgical supports and appliances. They can have fares to hospital refunded and their children can have free school meals. They may also be allowed special lump sums from time to time to replace clothing and bedding. When necessary they can have free legal aid and advice.

Supplementary benefit is non-contributory and not taxed, but it is very much means tested. People wishing to claim should complete the form in leaflet SB 1, obtainable from post offices and social security offices. Unemployed people should claim on form B 1 from unemployment benefit offices.

Mobility allowance

People under retirement age who are unable or virtually unable to walk are entitled to receive mobility allowance if their incapacity is likely to last for twelve months or more. They must also be likely to use it (not bed-ridden, for example). A flat-rate weekly payment is made to all who are entitled to it whether they receive other benefits or not. However, it cannot be paid at the same time as a vehicle allowance, or paid to owners of a DHSS vehicle, and it renders the recipient ineligible for the mobility addition to supplementary benefit.

Mobility allowance is intended to replace the issue of invalid tricycles (which for the benefit of the uninitiated are three-wheeled cars and *not* three-wheeled pedal cycles – however much the imagination may delight in the idea!) which are being phased out as they are unsafe. The allowance is non-contributory and not means tested, but it is taxable. It can be applied for on the form in leaflet NI 211 from social security offices.

Road tax exemption

A person who receives mobility allowance does not have to pay Vehicle Excise Duty (road tax) on a vehicle used by the disabled person himself. An application form is sent automatically to the person who receives the allowance, and he should take it to the local vehicle licensing office, which will then give him a "tax exempt" disc. A disabled passenger who is outside the age limits for mobility allowance, who is virtually unable to walk, and who needs constant attention, may claim exemption from road tax for a vehicle registered in his name. Applications should be made to DHSS Disablement Services Branch, Government Buildings, Warbeck Hill Road, Blackpool, Lancs FY5 3TA.

Motability

Motability is a charity set up at the government's request, to help people receiving the mobility allowance to obtain and run a car on reasonable terms. Disabled people can pay in their mobility allowance in return for the lease of a car over four years. The car will be maintained and repaired under the terms of the lease, but adaptations, running costs and accident repairs have to be met by the driver. Motability plans to introduce a hire-purchase scheme as well in the near future. Details of these services can be obtained from Motability, State House, High Holborn, London WC1R 4SX.

Attendance allowance

All severely physically or mentally handicapped people over the age of two years who need a lot of looking after by day and/or night qualify for this. People who need care by both day and night receive a larger sum. It is non-contributory, not means tested and not taxed, and should be claimed on the form in leaflet NI 205 from social security offices.

Invalid care allowance

This allowance is paid to men and single women of working age who cannot go to work because they are looking after a sick or handicapped person who is receiving attendance allowance. A married woman living with her invalid husband does not qualify, even if she gave up working to care for him, as the state assumes that he will maintain her. There is a lot of pressure being put upon the government by both feminist and disabled pressure groups to alter this state of affairs.

The allowance is non-contributory and not means tested, but is taxable. Claims should be submitted on the form in leaflet NI 212 from social security offices.

Help with rent and rates

All people on low incomes who are not receiving supplementary benefit can apply for rent and rate relief. Handicapped people are often entitled to a better subsidy than the able-bodied, and the presence of a handicapped member of the household should always be mentioned when applying. The nature of the relief differs with the type of housing:

1. tenants in privately rented property may apply for rent allowances and rate rebates;
2. council house tenants may apply for rent and rate rebates;
3. people living in their own houses may apply for rate rebates.

In addition, households with a disabled member may claim rate relief in respect of any room or amenity (such as extra bathroom, toilet, wheelchair space, garage or car port) used predominantly by a disabled person, and made necessary by his disability.

All of these concessions are administered by the local authorities and enquiries should be made at the local housing department offices or rates offices.

People receiving supplementary benefit have their rent and rates taken into account when their weekly sum is being decided, and therefore they are not entitled to rebates as well. People uncertain which concession will benefit them most should enquire at their local social security office, or ask for a visiting officer to call.

People in hospital

Some social security benefits are reduced when the claimant goes into hospital, and allowances for dependants can be deducted when a dependant goes into hospital. As most of these benefits are designed to help people to keep themselves at home, they cannot be paid in full to a person who is being fed and cared for in an NHS hospital.

Supplementary benefit is reduced as soon as the patient goes into hospital, though dependants at home are still provided for. For the first four weeks, no other benefits are reduced. After four weeks, attendance allowance stops. After eight weeks sickness, injury, widow's, invalidity and retirement pensions are affected. After twelve weeks, invalid care allowance ceases. The local social security office must be notified as soon as the claimant goes into hospital and should be given as much notice as possible of his date of discharge, so that benefits can begin to be paid again.

People in residential homes

Residents do not lose their state benefits when they go into homes, but are usually asked to contribute the greater part of their incomes towards their keep. They are usually left with a relatively small sum for personal expenses. Local authorities and voluntary bodies running homes vary somewhat in their demands for payment from residents.

225

Provision for physically handicapped people

Benefits for disabled people who are working

Disabled people who are working may still qualify for certain benefits, especially so if their income is low. Certain allowances for the disabled continue to be paid while the recipient is working.

Family income supplement

This scheme was introduced to help families where the breadwinner, though working, was earning a very low wage – perhaps even less than he or she could have been bringing home on social security benefits. Though not designed with the disabled in mind it can be a useful addition to the salaries of a lot of handicapped people, for they are often in badly paid jobs and have worse than average chances of promotion.

FIS is payable when the total income of the family is below a certain level, known as the prescribed amount. Families must have at least one child in order to qualify. Lone parents must be working at least 24 hours a week, and fathers of two-parent families must be working at least 30 hours, in order to qualify. (Parents working shorter hours should instead apply for supplementary benefit, which can be paid to part-time workers.)

Families on FIS are automatically entitled to free school meals, prescriptions, dental treatment, spectacles, milk and vitamins for expectant mothers, fares to hospital and legal aid and advice. The award is made for 52 weeks, irrespective of changes of circumstances, and has to be re-assessed and renewed after this time. FIS is non-contributory and not taxed. It is means tested but child benefits, mobility allowance, attendance allowance, rent allowances, part of war disablement pension and foster parent payments are disregarded. Claims should be made on the form in leaflet FIS 1 from post offices and social security offices, and should be accompanied by five weekly pay slips or two monthly salary slips, from the weeks immediately preceding the claim. When slips are not readily available, the claim should be submitted at once and the pay slips sent on as soon as they arrive, for claims cannot be back-dated.

Industrial disablement benefit

People who have been awarded industrial disablement benefit

226

still receive it if disabled but still able to work. Further details are given on p. 221. It is not taxed.

War disablement pension

This too can be paid to people who are working. It is not taxed. More details are given on p. 221.

Mobility allowance

Disabled people who are working are eligible for this and obtain it as shown on p. 223. It is not taxed.

Fares to work scheme

People who are registered as severely disabled under the Disabled Persons (Employment) Act 1944, who are unable to use public transport for all or part of the journey to work and who are therefore paying increased costs may be assisted with the cost of taxi fares to work. Monthly payments of three-quarters of taxi expenses are made. People receiving mobility allowance may be included in this scheme if they are temporarily or permanently unable to drive. Information can be obtained from the Disablement Resettlement Officer at the local Jobcentre or employment office.

Other benefits to low-paid workers

People who are not receiving supplementary benefit but who live on low incomes are sometimes eligible for exemption from NHS charges for prescriptions, dental treatment, spectacles and medical appliances. They may also be able to receive refund of fares to hospital, school meals for their children and free legal aid and advice should they require it. Applications should be made at the time, i.e. on collecting the prescription, or in making an appointment with the dentist. Quite a number of low-paid workers receive rent and rate rebates and rent allowances, which are dealt with on p. 224 above.

Benefits for the elderly disabled

Retirement pension

Most disabled people are elderly and therefore entitled to the retirement pension. Men aged 65 and over and women aged

60 and over who have paid national insurance contributions receive a pension when they retire from work. Married women can get a pension based on their husband's contributions, or may choose to have one in their own right (they can draw whichever is the larger). People five years over retirement age draw a pension whether they are working or not. Pensioners do not pay NHS prescription charges. Retirement pension is contributory and not means tested, but it is taxable. Claim forms are sent automatically to those about to retire.

Supplementary pension

Old age pensioners who do not have enough money to live on can be paid supplementary benefit on top of retirement pension. A lot of pensioners receive both. Details are given on p. 222 above.

Over-80 pension

Many of our oldest inhabitants do not have sufficient national insurance contributions to give them the full retirement pension, and there are still one or two people around who had already retired when the scheme was first introduced. People over 80 who do not receive retirement pension and who have lived in the United Kingdom for ten years are able to receive the over-80 pension. Rates are lower than those of the retirement pension, so it often has to be topped up with supplementary benefit. It is non-contributory but it is means tested and taxable. The application form in leaflet NI 184 can be used to apply, and it is to be obtained from social security offices.

Attendance allowance

Retired people can be paid the attendance allowance. Fuller details are given on p. 224 above.

War disablement pension

People can be paid this in addition to retirement pension. See p. 221.

Rent and rate rebates and allowances

These are given in detail on p. 224. Many old people are getting one or more of these concessions, which cannot be claimed in addition to supplementary benefit.

Residents of old people's homes

The remarks about residential homes on p. 225 above apply equally to old people's homes.

23 Holidays

People with handicaps often approach social services departments for advice and help with holiday arrangements. Under the terms of the Chronically Sick and Disabled Persons Act, local authorities should provide information and may also contribute all or part of the cost of the holiday. Provision varies from authority to authority both in terms of financial help and in organised holiday arrangements. Often there is a choice between a holiday grant, an organised holiday run by the local authority, or placement on some holiday run by another organisation.

When advising a disabled person about holiday arrangements it is essential to consider the reason for taking a holiday as well as the degree of disability possessed. The disabled person may simply want to go on holiday – alone or with companions – for the same reasons as anyone else, but may need to know which places are suitable for disabled people and how to go about getting there. Others are so dependent that they need to go to a holiday centre with full care facilities while their families have a break from looking after them. Parents of severely handicapped children will need breaks as well, especially if the child is mentally handicapped and has behaviour problems.

Holidays for disabled people who want to make their own arrangements

Some local authorities make grants towards the cost of privately arranged holidays for handicapped people who are not earning, or arrange special transport. There are also local charities who will make holiday grants, and the local social services department should have a list of these. For many, however, it is simply information that is required. There are several hotels and guest houses, leisure centres and holiday camps that are willing to accept disabled guests, and that have some of their bedrooms and all of their amenities accessible to wheelchair users. There are many more places accessible to people who, though ambulant, cannot manage long flights of stairs, and who need to be accommodated near to the toilet.

There are two guides to holiday amenities that are especially recommended to disabled people who wish to make their own holiday arrangements: *Holidays for the Physically Handicapped* (published by the Royal Association for Disability and Rehabilitation (RADAR), 25 Mortimer Street, London W1N 8AB (also available from major branches of W. H. Smith and Sons)) and the set of leaflets on holiday facilities prepared by The Spastics Society, 16 Fitzroy Square, London W1P 5HQ. Both list special holiday centres, special holidays run by voluntary organisations, self-catering holidays, special interest holidays, children's holidays and a list of ordinary hotels and holiday camps that welcome disabled guests.

Handicapped people who make their own arrangements should be advised to write early to the hotel of their choice stating their disabilities. Wheelchair users need to quote the width of their chairs and say how much room they need to manoeuvre in bedrooms, bathrooms and toilets. They should be certain to enquire if they can get from hotel to town or beach easily, for some hotels are on terraces high above the town and are effectively cut off from shops, beaches and theatres.

People who need help with personal care need to have someone with them on holiday and people who use special equipment should either take it with them or arrange to borrow it from the local branch of the British Red Cross Society or St John Ambulance Brigade. Some hotels can cater for the more usual special diets if they are given adequate warning beforehand and managers may be willing to have meals served in the guests' own rooms to people with eating difficulties.

Access guides have been drawn up for a number of towns in Britain, and also for Paris. All are available from RADAR and cost between 10p and 40p.

Special holiday homes and holiday schemes for the handicapped

Special holidays are organised for people who need a lot of help and for those who, though mildly handicapped, prefer a special holiday as they are uncertain of their ability to cope in an ordinary hotel. A lot of mildly disabled people are elderly and prefer to go on an organised holiday with a group because they have no one else to go with.

Local authorities and local and national voluntary bodies organise a wide range of schemes, some for their own members or residents only and some open to a wider clientèle. The publications mentioned in the previous section list a good many of these but most local social services departments have their own list of tried and tested arrangements, often with transport laid on. These schemes need to be booked into as early as possible, as demand is very great. There may also be a system of priorities operating.

It is essential to arrange the right sort of holiday for the right person. The severely handicapped person who needs nursing care will need to be found a place that provides plenty of entertainment as well, otherwise he or she could spend a lot of the holiday just sitting around. A lot of holidays are organised at holiday camps chartered specially outside the main holiday season, and if the weather is inclement then indoor activities are essential. It should be noted too that holiday camps in March and April are often not suitable for chest and heart patients who can become ill if exposed to too much wind and rain when moving between buildings, and subsequently have to spend most of their holiday in bed.

Handicapped holiday schemes can be divided roughly into those catering for severely handicapped people and those for people with less severe disabilities; for those where handicapped go alone and those where families and friends are welcome. Local authorities usually have some arrangement for paying all or part of the cost of the disabled person's holiday, but escorts are expected to pay the full fee. The cost is usually lower than the price of a normal hotel or holiday camp holiday.

Help for relatives nursing a severely handicapped person

Short-stay placements at nursing homes and special centres are available all the year round for those whose care places a severe burden upon their families. Local authorities who cannot accommodate such people locally in establishments of their own are expected to see that they are cared for elsewhere and that any costs are paid. Some local authorities take people into old people's homes for short stays, but this is not ideal for the younger disabled. The Spastics Society's *Holiday and Short Term Care Facilities* gives details of establishments designed to cater for handicapped people who need care, and which also have recreational amenities provided.

Holidays for handicapped children

Parents of handicapped children who need a rest from looking after them can send them to one of the holiday centres run by voluntary bodies in several parts of the country. These homes cater for a variety of needs. Some accept only the physically handicapped, others take mentally handicapped children. A few take multiply handicapped and emotionally disturbed children, too. There is always some form of entertainment provided and activities such as riding, swimming, games and outings are often on offer.

There are also some small units owned by local authorities designed to provide a break for parents while allowing the children to continue attending school. These are not strictly speaking holiday homes and should be seen as short-stay children's homes. Regular use of these to provide a break for the parents of severely handicapped teenagers could help to keep such children out of permanent care and it is a pity that more local authorities do not have them. The Spastics Society's leaflet *Family Help Units* lists a few homes of this type owned by various voluntary bodies. Payment can always be made for short-term care placements of children, under the provisions of the Children's Acts.

Social workers trying to find short-stay places for very handicapped children should not overlook the possibility of finding a foster home. There have been some very successful foster placements, even with multiply handicapped children. Local authorities have provision for paying higher than usual fees for fostering severely handicapped youngsters and it is worth making a case with one's own department to obtain the highest fee so as to keep good foster mums in circulation. Financial necessity can drive a lot of mothers out to work as soon as their own children are old enough and people who like fostering handicapped children are far too valuable to lose in this way.

Holidays abroad

There is no good reason why disabled people should not take their holidays abroad. Provided that they make enquiries beforehand and make adequate arrangements, people travelling alone or with friends and relatives can and do join in ordinary package holidays. However, in fairness to the staff of the holiday industry, they should enquire in plenty of time and be prepared to give full information about their limitations to the travel agent and tour organiser. RADAR has produced a most helpful booklet, *Booking a Holiday – Information for the Disabled Holiday Maker*, which sets out advice and information for physically handicapped people who want to holiday abroad. Their directory *Holidays for the Physically Handicapped* (item 49 in the Bibliography) includes information on holidays overseas. There are also a number of package tours abroad organised by clubs such as PHAB for their own members. The Spastics Society also organises package tours and will send details on request. For the very severely disabled, including those who need medical attention, "Across" organises continental tours by "Jumbulance" – a vehicle purpose built upon a bus chassis which contains curtained bunks as well as seats, toilet, cooker and fridge and medical equipment. Originally designed to take sick pilgrims to Lourdes, these vehicles are now also used for continental holiday purposes, and can also be hired, with drivers, by other groups of disabled people. Details are available from Across Trust, Crown House, Morden, Surrey SM4 5EW.

Travelling for disabled people

Air travel

The British Airports Authority has a series of leaflets covering each of their airports, giving information for disabled passengers. Each leaflet gives information and maps of the airport concerned and tells disabled people where to obtain assistance and where to find ramps, lifts and accessible toilets. These leaflets are obtainable from British Airports Publications, Brochure Department, Wellington Road, Cheriton, Folkestone, Kent.

Airlines have their own arrangements for looking after disabled air passengers but, if warned in advance, can ensure that people with walking difficulties or in wheelchairs can be met at airports and conveyed to and from their planes. Airlines may request medical details from the patient's own doctor before accepting people with some illnesses and disabilities on one of their flights. Folding wheelchairs are carried free of charge. Handicapped passengers might also like to send for *Care in the Air*, a booklet issued by the Airline Users' Committee, Space House, 43–59 Kingsway, London WC2B 6TE.

Travel by British Rail

British Rail staff are willing to assist disabled travellers at railway stations provided that they are told in advance that a disabled person intends to travel. People in wheelchairs are advised to contact the area manager at their departure station at least two days before travelling if possible, giving date and time of journey, departure and destination, any changes of train en route and mode of travel to the station. Staff will then arrange to meet the disabled person and escort him to his train. Those who do not normally use a wheelchair may arrange to borrow one if the station is large, and railway staff can use luggage lifts not normally open to passenger use. Railway staff will also escort disabled people between platforms during changes of train and will see them into their taxis or friends' vehicles at the other end of the journey. British Rail makes no charge for assistance of this kind.

Provided that they make arrangements with the station staff beforehand, disabled people who are not confined to a wheelchair, even though they may use one, can travel in an ordinary passenger seat and have their chair carried free in the guard's van (if it folds up and weighs less than 30 kg). If necessary they can be carried to their seat in a special carrying chair narrow enough to be taken along the train corridor. They pay the normal fare. Those who cannot leave their chairs may travel in the guard's van for half the second class fare for the journey. Travelling in the guard's van requires a special permit, applied for in advance. (Disabled people who need to travel daily to work may apply for a different permit, and may also buy a week's supply of tickets in advance to cut down time spent in queueing.)

The new Mark III first class carriages have wide doors which admit wheelchairs, and some removable seats that can be taken out to allow a wheelchair to occupy the space. These carriages are in service on only a few routes at the moment though British Rail hopes to introduce more before very long. Some high-speed trains have these carriages too. Passengers with wheelchairs using these coaches travel in first class carriages for half of the second class fare. Unfortunately, no British Rail carriage has or is likely to have toilets accessible to wheelchair users. The carrying chairs are in use only at stations, and should not be used when trains are in motion.

A useful leaflet, *British Rail and Disabled Travellers*, can be obtained from the Joint Committee on Mobility for the Disabled (Hon Sec. N. D. B. Elwes Esq.), Wanborough Manor, Wanborough, nr Guildford, Surrey GU3 2JR, on receipt of a stamped addressed envelope measuring 110 × 220 mm.

Travellers in London

Those taking a holiday in London should be advised to read *London for the Disabled* by Freda Bruce Lockhart (item 50 in the Bibliography). This book, well and entertainingly written, gives advice on parking, toilets, hotels, cafes, entertainments, shopping and sightseeing. It would be useful, too, to those passing through London, for it gives information on access to the main railway stations and air terminals.

Underground travel is not accessible to disabled people in wheelchairs, or to the ambulant disabled unable to manage stairs and escalators. London buses have seats designated for ambulant disabled and elderly travellers, but strangers to London should be warned that travel by London bus is unbelievably slow, vehicles appearing to stop at every lamp-post!

24 Recreation and leisure

People with handicaps often have a lot of time on their hands and have greater than average difficulty in occupying it. As most of the disabled are elderly, and many of the younger ones are unemployed, they have less money to spend on entertainment than the rest of the population. Deprived of work, people may need not only to occupy their time, but also to develop their creativity and enliven their intellects. It is not surprising therefore that occupation for the disabled is something with which the helping professions are often asked to assist. The problems, and some of the possible solutions, are given below.

Disabled people needing organised activities

The Chronically Sick and Disabled Persons Act clearly lays down a duty upon local authorities to provide leisure-time occupations for the disabled. Though the exact interpretation of this part of the Act is left to local authority discretion, there should always be a variety of services available to meet local need and demand. Staff working with disabled people should familiarise themselves with local amenities (including those organised by voluntary bodies) so that they can help individuals choose the activity best suited to their interests and abilities.

Most local authority social services departments run day centres, which range from drop-in clubs for tea and a chat, through craft centres and classes to well-equipped workshops for manufacturing and packaging goods. Industrial work carries a small wage but, except in sheltered workshops (dealt with in Chapter 21), does not aim to provide more than pin-money. Work centres, by their very nature, cannot make a

237

profit and remuneration is kept below the level at which pensions and unemployment benefits could be affected. Craftwork, when good enough, sells well, but never justifies the man-hours spent on production. It should therefore be considered a hobby with pin-money rather than a commercial enterprise, and be valued for its intellectual stimulus. All centres need to provide transport for the less ambulant clients.

Clubs for the elderly and the disabled aim only to entertain and can often offer board games, competitions, bingo, paid performers, parties and outings according to the enterprise of the people running them, who are often voluntary workers. Again, transport is usually provided.

Those who cannot leave the house easily, or who live a long way from any centre, will often benefit from the visits of a handicraft instructor. These underpaid and unsung heroines of the social services are often the only visitors lonely old people ever see, and they teach crafts, supply materials to the proficient and help to arrange sales of finished goods. The sort of crafts popular with disabled people include knitting, crochet, soft-toy making, weaving, rug-work, leatherwork, macramé, rush, cane-basketry, stool-seating and mosaic tiling. The instructor can usually suggest activities that enhance the abilities of the client, and suggest ways of overcoming disabilities so as to encourage choice of crafts in which individuals can do worthwhile work, and develop their creativity.

People in residential homes may well need this sort of activity. In addition, they need a change of scene, fresh company and outside interests as well, so visits, outings and *individual* membership of interest groups are to be encouraged.

All housebound people should be reminded of the mobile library service, in which books can be brought to the disabled person's home by staff of the local public library. The vans carry a good selection of books and special requests can often be met.

Activity holidays and special activity clubs

There are special activity holiday schemes run by local and national charities which are especially suitable for the disabled person who wants to try something different. Many are organised by The Spastics Society, PHAB and RADAR, all of which issue information about their own, and some of the other, schemes. Their addresses are given in Chapter 11.

Activity holidays are specially organised for the disabled in purpose-built or adapted accommodation, and tuition is given by experts in their own subjects. Drama, music, art, pottery, photography, film-making, puppetry and natural history are among the most popular activities. Other centres specialise in sport and offer swimming, canoeing, sailing, riding and skiing.

For those wishing to pursue some sporting activity in their own home areas, there are local sport clubs for the disabled offering riding, swimming, archery and angling. Some competitive sports are segregated for the sake of fair competition. Special clubs for the disabled can also provide a place to learn a new skill before joining a club run by the able-bodied. Information on local and national sporting amenities can be had from the British Sports Association for the Disabled (address in Chapter 11), which is the national co-ordinating body.

Disabled people pursuing their own interests independently

Although the elderly or more severely handicapped may need to have their recreational amenities provided for them, it is always best when those who can pursue their own interests alongside the rest of the population. The problems here are, of course, access and attitudes. Access problems are discussed in detail elsewhere, but it is relevant to point out that access problems can be quoted as an excuse to exclude the disabled from groups whose members are uncertain of their ability to include a handicapped person. It may take a good deal of persistence, patience and tact for a disabled person to succeed among the able-bodied, but once he has done it, others will be accepted after him. Most crafts, table-top hobbies, music and cultural societies can offer full participation to a disabled member. Local adult education departments offer a wide variety of day and evening classes and, again, many disabled could join in if they so wished. Most local authorities put an accent on integrated classes and make sure that at least some premises are easily accessible to disabled people.

Some people have disabilities that do not preclude membership of open sporting clubs, and the best guide to possible activities is the booklet published by the Disabled Living Foundation called *Outdoor Pursuits for Disabled People* by Norman Croucher (item 47 in the Bibliography). See also the appropriate section in *Directory for the Disabled*. Many disabled people – including amputees – swim well, one-legged people have been known to water-ski, people with one impaired foot can row boats, amputees can fly aeroplanes and gliders and virtually anybody – even the handless – can go fishing from a river bank.

The disabled person who likes "doing his own thing" will get on and do it unaided, but might nevertheless appreciate some information on amenities, from time to time, and some encouragement to overcome the inevitable problems of acceptance by other people.

25 Residential homes

The circumstances leading up to the decision that a person needs to go into a residential home because he can no longer continue to live a satisfactory life in his own home are many and varied. The decision can be made at any age and will often depend on the occurrence of a particular event or culmination of a set of circumstances.

The circumstances

Some of the circumstances are:

1. Death of the caring relative, leaving the disabled person without adequate means of support. This will of course be coupled with the psychological reactions of bereavement, which may force the decision upon the person or those responsible for him. This happens most frequently with elderly people who have had elderly partners or with the severely handicapped adult who has been looked after by elderly parents.
2. Rejection by the caring relative. Rejection is often considered as a totally negative response but there will often have been a long period of time where the relative has provided total care but can realistically no longer continue to do so, either because of her own failing abilities or a "reaching the end of her tether". This reaction may accompany a corresponding deterioration in the health of the disabled person.
3. Deterioration mentally and/or physically of a disabled person living alone to the extent that he can no longer look after himself adequately and is no longer motivated to do so.

In all of the above situations support may have been given by community nurses and social services staff but this support has now become inadequate in meeting the person's needs.

4. Sudden onset of severe disability, e.g. stroke or quadriplegia, in a person who is either living alone or with relatives who will be unable to look after him. The disabled person may for these reasons be unable even to return home from hospital for a temporary period prior to admission to a residential home.
5. A young disabled person may feel the need to leave his home and his parents in order to assert his independence. A residential home may be the best alternative if he is too severely disabled to care for himself in an unattended situation such as in a flat, and the home may provide all the facilities which he needs, including work.
6. There is always the circumstance where a disabled person may decide that he will feel much less isolated in a residential home than in his own home, even when he is living with his family. He may also feel that he would rather leave than tolerate his feelings of guilt and unhappiness because he knows he is a burden to them and his relationship with them has deteriorated.

These reasons for choosing residential care are, of course, simplified. Every individual's set of circumstances will be different and will call for a very individual approach to his problem.

Who makes the decision?

Ideally the disabled person himself should be provided with enough information to decide for himself and the opportunity to choose when and where he should go. The decision is usually easier when he has visited residential homes, either for holiday periods or on a visit to see the home and the staff, and has been given time to consider the advantages and disadvantages. However, time may be of the essence and an urgent decision required. If the onset of his disability has been sudden then he may have to decide from hospital because he is unable to return to his own home. The decision may be made by others, his doctor or his family, with very short notice being given to him to consider his future. The idea that to let the person know too early will upset him is taking all choice away and making it more unlikely that he will accept the residential home in the short term or even the long term.

A decision may have to be made suddenly following the death of or rejection by his supporting relative. Every effort should be made to avoid sudden and irreversible decisions on residential care. A temporary solution can often be found to allow sufficient time for the person to prepare himself and for the most suitable accommodation to be found.

When a person's health is deteriorating, where there is stress and anxiety on the part of the family, friends and professionals, and where it seems likely that leaving home for residential care will be required in the future, then the social worker may decide upon an open discussion of this alternative with the disabled person at an early stage so that he can make plans on his own behalf.

What can a residential home offer?

The severely disabled person at home may find his time totally taken up with the satisfaction of his physiological needs, eating, toileting, sleeping and his own personal needs for safety. There is often little or no hope of being able to satisfy his other needs for social contact, creative fulfilment or the realisation of his own personal potential for development. This is particularly so when he is living alone and endeavouring to look after himself, with considerable physical and psychological effort.

Residential homes take care of physiological and safety needs by helping the person where necessary and so allowing him time to develop social, recreational and leisure pursuits as well as, in some homes, a normal work routine. With these facilities considered as important, residents can take part in running the home, planning social and recreational events, transport for journeys out and holidays. Also because they are living in close proximity to others, there is often more opportunity for making close relationships. For example, young people in Spastics Society homes frequently make deep relationships which may lead to marriage, and sometimes to the ability to leave the residential home together to set up house in the community. Many residential homes, in particular the Cheshire Homes, provide counselling staff and social workers for residents.

243

A number of homes have workshop facilities attached where creative and work activities are provided for residents. These provide a focus for contact with the surrounding community which is important if residents are to benefit from a life which is integrated with that of able-bodied people as far as is possible.

Provision and selection of residential care

The Social Research Branch of the DHSS is currently researching residential care for physically handicapped adults and has found that there are approximately 250 residential establishments in England which are run by the National Health Service, local authorities and voluntary agencies. The NHS establishments are mostly attached to hospitals and most often cater for the middle to older age groups of those who have become disabled during their adult life. They rarely provide for congenitally disabled people. Local authority homes usually provide for younger adults of average age around 30, many of whom are disabled from birth. Voluntary homes tend to provide for the same age range as the NHS, but a few are specifically for younger adults. The main provider in the voluntary sector is the Cheshire Foundation, with fifty-seven homes in England. The Spastics Society administers approximately thirty homes. Other providers include the Shaftesbury Society, Queen Elizabeth's Foundation for the Disabled and the Multiple Sclerosis Society of Great Britain.

Selection of a suitable residential home will depend upon whether it is necessary for the person to remain near to his own home, family and friends. It will also depend upon the age of the person and the age range of the home and what facilities the home provides in relation to the person's personality and interests. Just because there is a convenient local home, it will not necessarily be suited to the disabled person. Ideally, the opportunity should be given to the person to select the home which seems to him most suitable but there may be difficulties because of the lack of places.

All homes provide the opportunity for admission for a trial period of up to two years, as it is only by living there that a person can decide if he is going to be happy to make it his home. It should also be borne in mind that because a person goes into a home at, say, the age of 25, he will not necessarily want to stay there for the rest of his life. He may wish to move to another part of the country. This should be possible, but in practice, finance is a very important factor: most people are financed in residential homes by their local authority and it is often difficult to arrange for the transfer of a person to another home if the cost will be increased – that is, if he wants to move to a more expensive home. It would seem sensible, on this reasoning, not to select the cheapest home simply because it is the cheapest, for then it will be much more difficult, whoever is paying, to move to another place!

Bibliography

General

1. *The Handicapped Person in the Community*, ed. D. M. Boswell and J. M. Wingrove (Tavistock Publications in association with the Open University Press, 1974).
   Available from Open University Educational Enterprises Ltd, 12 Cofferidge Close, Stony Stratford, Milton Keynes MK11 1BY.

2. *Integrating the Disabled*: Report of the Snowdon Working Party (National Fund for Research into Crippling Diseases, 1976).
   Available from the publishers at Vincent House, 1 Springfield Road, Horsham, West Sussex RH12 2PB.

3. *Directory for the Disabled*, by A. Darnbrough and D. Kinrade (2nd edition, Woodhead-Faulkner, 1979).
   A reference book including a wide range of information for disabled people.

4. *An ABC of Services and Information for Disabled People*, by Barbara Macmorland (Disablement Income Group Charitable Trust, 1977).
   Available from the DIG, Attlee House, Toynbee Hall, 28 Commercial Street, London E1 6LR.

5. *Can Disabled People Go Where You Go?*: Report by the Silver Jubilee Committee on Improving Access for Disabled People (DHSS, 1979).
   Available from HMSO.

6. *People with Handicaps need Better-trained Workers*: CCETSW Paper 5 (Central Council for Education and Training in Social Work, 1974).
   Available from the council at Derbyshire House, St Chads Street, London WC1H 8AD.

246

7. *Stigma*, by Erving Goffman (Penguin, 1970).

8. *Asylums*, by Erving Goffman (Penguin, 1970).

9. *Institutional Neurosis*, by Russell Barton (Wright & Sons, 1976).

10. *Equipment for the Disabled* (Oxford Regional Health Authority on behalf of DHSS).
Set of books, each on a particular activity, e.g. Wheelchairs, Personal Care, Disabled Mother, Housing and Furniture.
Available from 2 Foredown Drive, Portslade, Brighton BN4 2BB.

11. Information lists on equipment for the disabled, published by the Disabled Living Foundation.
Regularly up-dated definitive lists of equipment which are invaluable to the social services worker. An annual fee is payable by departments which entitles them to be placed on the mailing list for up-dated sections of the lists.

Disabling diseases

12. *Davidson's Principles and Practice of Medicine*, ed. John McLeod (Churchill Livingstone, 1975).

13. *Clinical Neurology*, by F. A. Elliott (2nd edition, W. B. Saunders, 1971).

14. *The Stroke Patient: principles of rehabilitation*, by M. Johnstone (Churchill Livingstone, 1976).

15. *The Muscular Dystrophy Handbook* (Muscular Dystrophy Group of Great Britain, 1979).
Available from Nattrass House, 35 Macaulay Road, London SW4 0QP.

16. *Spina Bifida: the treatment and care of spina bifida children*, by Nancy Allum (George Allen & Unwin, 1975).

17. *So You're Paralysed*, by Bernadette Fallon (Spinal Injuries Association, 1975).

18. *Spina Bifida and Hydrocephalus* (BASW Publications, 1975).
Available from 16 Kent Street, Birmingham B5 6RD.

19. *Heart Trouble in the Family*, by Henrietta Chater-Jack (Health Horizon Ltd, 1970).

20. *The Wheelchair Child*, by Philippa Russell (Souvenir Press Ltd, 1978).

21. *Assessment of the Elderly Patient*, by F. I. Caird and T. C. Judge (2nd edition, Pitman Medical, 1979).

22. *Practical Management of the Elderly*, by W. Ferguson Anderson (Blackwell Scientific Publications, 1971).

23. *Psychogeriatrics*, by Brice Pitt (Churchill Livingstone, 1975).

24. *The Handicapped Child: assessment and management*, by Grace E. Woods (Blackwell Scientific Publications, 1975).

Rehabilitation

25. *Rehabilitation Today*, ed. Stephen Mattingly (Update Publications, 1977).

26. *Rehabilitation of the Severely Disabled*, by P. J. R. Nichols, Vol. 1. *Evaluation of a Disabled Living Unit*, Vol. 2. *Management* (Butterworth, 1971).

27. *Lifting, Moving and Transferring Patients*, by M. J. Rantz and D. Courtial (C. V. Mosby, 1977).

28. *Handling the Handicapped*, Chartered Society of Physiotherapy (2nd edition, Woodhead-Faulkner, 1980).

29. *A Stroke in the Family*, by Valerie Eaton Griffith (Penguin Books, 1970).

30. *Help Yourself: a handbook for hemiplegics and their families*, by Peggy Jay and others (3rd edition, Ian Henry Publications for RADAR, 1979).

31. *Clothing for the Handicapped Child* (Disabled Living Foundation, 1971).

32. *Clothes Sense* (Disabled Living Foundation, 1973).

33. *Footwear for Problem Feet* (Disabled Living Foundation, 1973).

34. *Early Days – You and Your Baby – Advice for Disabled Mothers* (Disabled Living Foundation, 1975).

35. *Kitchen Sense – for Disabled and Elderly People* (revised edition, Disabled Living Foundation, 1976).

36. *How to Talk to the Elderly Deaf*, by D. L. Fisch (published by the Health Department, Tottenham Town Hall, London N15).

37. *Incontinence*, by Dorothy Mandelstam (Heinemann Health Books, 1977).

Sexual advice

38. *Not Made of Stone: the sexual problems of handicapped people*, by K. Heslinga, A. M. C. M. Scheller and A. Verleugh (Woodhead-Faulkner, 1977).

39. *The Sexual Side of Handicap: a guide for the caring professions*, by W. F. R. Stewart (Woodhead-Faulkner, 1979).

40. *Sexual Aspects of Social Work*, by W. F. R. Stewart (Woodhead-Faulkner, 1979).

41. *Entitled to Love*, by Wendy Greengross (Malaby Press, 1976).

42. *The Joy of Sex*, by Alex Comfort (Mitchell Beazley/Quartet Books, 1974).

43. *More Joy of Sex*, by Alex Comfort (Mitchell Beazley/Quartet Books, 1974).

44. *Sex Manners for Men*, Robert Chartham (New English Library, 1968).

45. *Mainly for Wives*, by Robert Chartham (Tandem Paperbacks), 1964).

The preceding four books are not written specifically for disabled people but are nonetheless helpful.

Housing
46. *Designing for the Disabled*, by Selwyn Goldsmith (RIBA Publications, 1977).

47. *Design of Housing for the Convenience of Disabled People*: BS 5619 (British Standards Institution, 1978).

Holidays and leisure
47. *Outdoor Pursuits for Disabled People*, by Norman Croucher (Disabled Living Foundation, 1974).

48. *Have Wheels, Will Travel: disabled students on a study tour of Rome*, ed. Rachel Bleackley (Educational Explorers Reading/ Open University Press, 1976).
Available from Open University Educational Enterprises Ltd, 12 Cofferidge Close, Stony Stratford, Milton Keynes MK11 1BY.

49. *Holidays for the Physically Handicapped* (updated annually) (published by the Royal Association for Disability and Rehabilitation, 25 Mortimer Street, London W1N 8AB).

50. *London for the Disabled*, by Freda Bruce Lockhart (Ward Lock, 1973).

51. *The Easy Path to Gardening* (Disabled Living Foundation, 1972).

Residential homes

52. *A Life Apart: a pilot study of residential institutions for the physically handicapped and the young chronic sick*, by E. J. Miller and G. V. Gwynne (Tavistock Publications, 1972).
    Available from 11 Fetter Lane, London EC4.

53. *Counselling in a Residential Setting*, by R. Dawson-Shepherd and G. Corney (published in DHSS *'Social Work Service'* No. 19, March 1979).
    Available from DHSS, Alexander Fleming House, London SE1 6BY.

Index

251